FitFaith

*A Full 7 Week Devotional Journal
For a Healthier Life*

Susan Kelley

ISBN-13: 978-1511612463
ISBN-10: 1511612460

GREETINGS

At the age of 33, I realized that I was obese, unhappy, and unhealthy. With the help of my friends, family, and most of all, my Jesus, I now have a transformed life. As of the date of this writing, I have lost 90 pounds and have maintained that weight loss. I have written this little 7 week devotional in hopes of inspiring you as well. *You* too can make a transformation if you allow Jesus to start His work.

Why seven weeks? The number seven is the number of completion, and there are seven days in a week.

The transformed life, both spiritual and physical, is a permanent one. Seven days and seven weeks is a reminder that this new life that I now walk is a permanent and complete change! And I'm so grateful!

This book is dedicated to Jesus my Savior, who has transformed my life in ways I never could've imagined.

Week 1, Day 1: Confidence

Philippians 4:13 *"For I can do everything with the help of Christ who gives me the strength I need."* NLT

I was sure I couldn't do it. The desire was there, but I had never had much luck before. My life just wasn't conducive to the time needed to commit to exercise, I had kids who would balk at the sight of healthy food, and I just didn't know if I had the long-term discipline needed to go on for as long as I knew it would take. I watched television shows about people who had lost large amounts of weight, but they were on TV for a purpose. These were not your ordinary, every-day type of people, after all, if they were on TV. They had celebrity trainers, they had unlimited budgets, and there was support there for them! I didn't have any of those things, and I certainly didn't even have the guts it would take to show the world how I had failed physically. I had no confidence in myself to complete just one workout, let alone day after day of it.

Paul is giving some closing remarks to the Philippian church in this epistle. He thanks them for the gift of support they had sent him, and praises God for always providing everything he needs. There have been times that Paul has been without, even hungry and with no resources. Yet God supplied, and He supplied generously. Paul then states that he can do anything because God gives him strength. Because of Christ, Paul can continue spreading the Gospel, keeping on, no matter what the circumstances.

The confidence in myself has always been very little. Over the course of my life, I've allowed Satan to plant seeds of doubt in me, always sure that I couldn't succeed at whatever the task that was before me. As I allowed those seeds of doubt to grow, sometimes I would get so overwhelmed and overcome with fear and doubt that I would succumb to deep depression, confident only of the fact that I was a failure. Self-confidence itself seemed so far away, and yet, here was a Scripture telling me the contrary.

If Paul, a former persecutor of Christians, can press on, preaching the Gospel, how come I have doubts? Why can't I simply take care of the body God has given me?

As the weeks turned into months, and the months have now turned into years, I realize that I can't have confidence in myself. I have no confidence in myself because I alone am not able. But He is. Because Christ lives in me, works through me, and gives me strength, I can do anything. I need only ask and depend on Him!

The writer of Hebrews says in 4:16, *"So let us come boldly to the throne of our gracious God. There we will receive his mercy, and we will find grace to help us when we need it most."* NLT

Christ is our His Priest, desires for us to lean on Him and to find our strength in Him. He is faithful to bestow upon us His grace. We may not have any confidence in ourselves, but with Him, all things are possible!

Encouragement for Today
Psalm 27:3 *"Though a mighty army surrounds me, my heart will not fear. Even if they attack me, I remain confident."* NLT

Ephesians 3:12 *"Because of Christ and our faith in him, we can now come fearlessly into God's presence, assured of his glad welcome."* NLT

> I need confidence in God!
> His power, His Resources
> His provisions of self
> control.
>
> Help me Lord to Rely on
> you for self control -
> I don't need to generate
> it myself

Week 1, Day 2: Embarrassment

Psalm 139:13-17 *"You made all the delicate, inner parts of my body and knit me together in my mother's womb. Thank you for making me so wonderfully complex! Your workmanship is marvelous -- and how well I know it. You watched me as I was being formed in utter seclusion, as I was woven together in the dark of the womb. You saw me before I was born. Every day of my life was recorded in your book. Every moment was laid out before a single day had passed. How precious are your thoughts about me, O God! They are innumerable"* NLT

The last place I wanted to be was a gym. I am a natural introvert and much prefer the company of only Jesus and me on most occasions. Overweight, feeling ugly, and a never-before athlete, I did not belong in a gym. My husband tried his best to encourage me, assuring me that I didn't have to go to a gym. I could walk outside, ride a bicycle, and work up to jogging! So I tried. I remembered how to ride a bicycle and even remembered enjoying it as a child. We set out with our two children on our newly purchased bicycles to ride just around the block. By the second turn, my stomach was burning, my lungs were, I was sure, about to explode, my thighs felt like bricks, and I was sweating. This was not the way I thought this would turn out. I clumsily pedaled home, crying, discouraged, and positive that everyone in the neighborhood witnessed my fail at physical activity. I just wasn't cut out for this, and I'd only made it around the block! This....this was embarrassing! And it just wasn't the neighbors. My husband was physically fit, my kids of course, had ridden bikes for years, and they weren't even winded! I however was convinced I was about to die!

In this psalm, David acknowledges that the Lord knows him well, knowing every thought he thinks, every word he says, and every feeling he experiences. The Lord totally understands! But then, we see a beautiful word picture of the Master creator, who has created us *wonderfully*. God loves humanity so much that He chose to create us in His image. And that means you too! What's more, His works are wonderful! God, in His holy nature, is incapable of making less than perfection. Again, this means you!

I purchased this verse as a wall sticker for the bathroom of my children. I want them to grow up, remembering every time they look in the mirror, that they are created by the Master. He doesn't make mistakes, and He thinks you're beautiful...just the way you are.

While we may be embarrassed at our lack of fitness at first, we must remember that we are no less than God-created. His thoughts are precious of you, and that's all that matters.

Take a few moments and read the entire Psalm. Press in.

Encouragement for Today
Genesis 1:27 *"So God created people in his own image; God patterned them after himself; male and female he created them."* NLT

1 John 3:1a *"Behold, what manner of love the Father hath bestowed upon us, that we should be called the sons of God:"* KJV

Romans 8:1 *"There is therefore now no condemnation to them which are in Christ Jesus, who walk not after the flesh, but after the Spirit."* KJV

Even c all my imperfections, He Loves me. - & loves to call me his child.

Week 1, Day 3: Counting the Cost

Luke 14:28 *But don't begin until you count the cost. For who would begin construction of a building without first calculating the cost to see if there is enough money to finish it?* NLT

I start my day the same way every day. As soon as I wake up, because I'm not a coffee drinker, I go mix my fruit-punch spark (my secret weapon), and I sip it while I spend time with my Jesus. After that, I grab my laptop and go to my favorite website. No, it's not social media. It's my online food/activity/weight tracker. I enter everything I plan to do that day on the activity tab and it calculates how many calories I will burn that day, based on my height, current weight, and activity level. I also make a meal plan for myself that day, based on family/work plans, and it calculates my nutrition as well. This tracker helps me keep on track to know whether I'm eating too much, eating too little, not moving enough, and even if I'm deficient in a vitamin! This thing is detailed!

As we go through our fitness journey and live healthy lives, it's always a great idea to get a solid picture of where we stand. Recording your nutrition, exercise, and weight/measurements helps us stay on track and remain focused.

In Luke's Gospel, he records an instance when Jesus was becoming very popular. Jesus though cautions the crowds that the cost of being his disciple was very high. He tells them to count the cost, deciding if it's something they're willing to risk and in which to invest. Throughout the gospels, we read what those disciples gave up to follow Him and then to spread the Gospel after His resurrection. They were cast into prison, tortured, beaten, and martyred for following Jesus. Following Jesus can cost us relationships, careers, social standing, and most of all, our very lives. The question then is, "Is He worth it?"

Think of the "investment" that God, our Father, made when He sent His only Son to die as the atoning sacrifice for the redemption of the entire world! And after all Jesus has sacrificed for us, how can we respond in any other way than all-in. Yes, salvation is a free-gift, but being His disciple will cost you! I can assure you that following Jesus, being His disciple, is always worth it, but it is an eternal-investment. The cost is never too high.

Living a healthy life takes both an initial and a long-term

investment. It's time consuming to spend time working out and planning meals. From a financial standpoint, we may invest in gym memberships, workout clothes, and vitamin supplements. But part of being a disciple is caring for His creation. The investment we make pays off big time while we care for our bodies to better serve our Master!

Spend a few minutes reading through Luke 14:25-35. Consider the cost!

Encouragement for Today
Proverbs 20:25 *"Don't trap yourself by making a rash promise to God and only later counting the cost."* NLT

Luke 14:33 *"In the same way, any of you who do not give up everything he has cannot be my disciple."* NLT

I don't set high goals because I doubt my own self to fulfil them + I don't ever think of asking God for help in meeting any goals.

Today, I haven't felt hungry! Very weird for me. Thank you Lord.

Week 1, Day 4: Preparation

Matthew 24:43 *"Understand this: If a homeowner knew exactly when a burglar was coming, he would keep watch and not permit his house to be broken into. You also must be ready all the time, for the Son of Man will come when least expected."* NLT

Nothing to eat! I had just come home from work on a hot, humid summer day and was trying to make dinner plans. Nothing sounded good, and I was tired. Normally organized, I would at least make a mental plan for dinner earlier in the day so that things wouldn't take so long once I'd arrived home. But today there was no mental plans happening outside of mortgage escrow, my current profession. There was no meat thawed, my lettuce was wilted, and I was tempted to just order pizza. That had been my go-to before...before I asked Jesus to help me, I thought. I had asked for Him to take control of this area of my life only a week before, and now here I was, considering pizza of all things.

I had prayed prayers many times before over a pizza dinner. "Lord bless this food to the nourishment of our bodies, and our bodies to your service." It's laughable now that we pray those kinds of prayers. If that's the food that's provided, then by all means be thankful for it. But in reality, we somehow spiritualize our bad eating choices and ask God to magically change the molecular structure! That night, there was a first prayer uttered that hasn't gone unrepeated since. "Lord, please help me resist the temptation for pizza." In that moment, I'm not kidding, God brought to mind a recipe I had read a few days before, and most of the ingredients were already on hand. I just had to run out to get a couple of things around the corner.

I was thankful that God had delivered me from the temptation, but inside I was frustrated at myself for the huge struggle that had just occurred in my head. I realized that if I had only prepared ahead of time, the temptation wouldn't have been so great.

Preparation is truly the key. Every week before I go grocery shopping, I jot down a quick meal list so I at least have a rough plan in mind for things to buy. Having healthy ingredients on hand and readily at my disposal vastly cuts down on resorting to a quick fix in a drive-thru. Personally, every day, I make an eating plan for myself, calculating my nutrition and activity so I know how I'm doing and ensure that I'm able to stand against temptation. I even go so far as to cut up things like cantaloupe and watermelon and put them in a bowl in the refrigerator so they are quickly available when my sweet tooth takes over. I boil a few eggs every few days, peel them, and put them in a plastic baggie in the refrigerator. But things happen. Work takes longer than normal that day, traffic is backed-up, or someone gets sick, and we end up having to fill a need quickly. If we have yogurt cups, fruit, and almonds on hand, trust me, we can be ready for anything!

In our text today, we see Jesus speaking about His second coming. He speaks of the time when the Son of Man will come back for His church, and no one knows the time or the hour. The Scripture says that, unexpectedly, He will appear to claim those who have been faithful, and there are those who will be unprepared. Those who have not accepted Him as their Savior and have not lived a life pleasing to Him will be left. The Day of Judgment is coming, and no one knows the day or time. People who spend much time trying to figure out when/where He's coming are only spinning their wheels and wasting valuable time. We must simply be prepared. That's all He asks. Trust Him as your Savior and live a life pleasing to Him! Share Him with others so that they may be prepared too. When He comes, we'll wish we had done more.

Are you prepared? Have you accepted Him as your Savior, or are you thinking that you've still got time? The Scripture is clear. *"The Son of Man will come when least expected."*

Take some time today to read through Matthew chapters 24-25. He's coming!

Encouragement for Today:
2 Timothy 2:15 *"Work hard so that you can present yourself to God and receive his approval. Be a good worker, one who does not need to be ashamed and who correctly explains the word of truth."* NLT

Matthew 7:13-14 *"You can enter God's Kingdom only through the narrow gate. The highway to hell is broad, and its gate is wide for the many who choose that way. But the gateway to life is very narrow and the road is difficult, and only a few ever find it."* NLT

1 Corinthians 2:9b *"No eye has seen, no ear has heard, and no mind has imagined what God has prepared for those who love him."* NLT

Week 1, Day 5: Life-Giving Water

John 4:14 *But whoever drinks of the water that I will give him will never be thirsty again. The water that I will give him will become in him a spring of water welling up to eternal life.* ESV

I've never been a big drinker. I mean, a drinker of *any* liquid. When I was a child, my parents stopped ordering a drink for me when we visited restaurants because I simply wouldn't drink it. As I grew older, the need for beverages still largely eluded me because I didn't see the point of gulping down water or soda unless I was thirsty. It honestly never crossed my mind.

When I was 14 years old, our area experienced a major ice storm that knocked out the power to our home as well as the water plant for 21 days. As a 14 year old that still had to go to school (it had working utilities), this was a major problem. I quickly realized the importance of water. We needed it for personal hygiene, to wash clothes, to cook, and to clean. Everywhere I looked, the need for water screamed at us.

When I started my fitness journey, I soon realized the need for water. When I was exerted, I was thirsty. When I was hot, I needed it to help cool me down. Every weight-loss blog and fitness guru I saw stressed the importance of drinking half your body weight in ounces. And so I drank. I calculated the ounces I drank on my little handy app on my phone, and I carefully kept track so as not to deprive my body. It worked! I still drink water and monitor it today as I do my best to maintain a healthy lifestyle. Every part of our body needs water to nourish it in order for our bodies to work properly. We can diet and exercise every day, but if we are dehydrated, the weight will simply not come off.

Water is central to life. There's no getting around it, and there's no getting by without it. In ancient times, cities were planned and built around sources of water...except for Samaria. Jesus travels through there on His way to Galilee, and stops at the historic Jacob's well. There He meets a woman drawing water. It was an unusual time of day for her to be drawing water, as most women would perform this chore earlier in the day, so as to avoid the worst heat. Not her. She normally kept isolated from others because of her tainted past, which is why she was shocked when a Jewish man spoke to her. Not only that, but he offers her *living water.* Now she is really perplexed. Here is a Jewish man, in Samaria of all places, offering her *living water.* The thought on her mind is, "Samaria doesn't have a river. How can he offer me something that's not here? That's impossible!" Oh, but she didn't know the life that Jesus was offering. That day, this previously sinful woman's life was changed. She ran back to the village, telling everyone that the Messiah was there...and He offered living water. Not only that, verse 39 of this chapter says, "Many Samaritans from the village believed in Jesus..." because of the testimony of this woman.

Are you thirsty? Has your spiritual life been neglected? Are you parched? Jesus longs to fill you with His life-giving, living water. Spend some time today reading John 4:1-42 and receive this gift He longs to give you.

Encouragement for Today
John 7:38 *"Whoever believes in me, as the Scripture has said, 'Out of his heart will flow rivers of living water."* ESV

Isaiah 44:3 *"For I will pour water on the thirsty land, and streams on the dry ground; I will pour my Spirit upon your offspring, and my blessing on your descendants."* ESV

I wouldn't say my life is like parched ground, but maybe some areas are. I do need water thrown over one area + pray for that.

an unrelated event happened last night. Eating out c̄ the BD Club, I ate the whole meal cause 2 others ordered same thing + quickly ate theirs. I didn't want them to feel bad, so I ate all of mine even tho I was full + could to have stopped earlier. I need

stop that + do what is right for me

13

Week 1, Day 6: Setting Goals

Philippians 3:13b-14 *"Forgetting what is behind and straining toward what is ahead, I press on toward the goal to win the prize for which God has called me heavenward in Christ Jesus."* NIV

Throughout my adult years, I always laughed about how I had weighed 135 pounds in junior high school, but that number was totally unattainable. I would shop for clothing and skip the misses section altogether. Straight to the plus sized selections I'd go, inwardly feeling discouraged and hating the thought of having to try on yet another bigger size than the last time. They were just making clothes different than they used to, I'd reason to myself.

"If I could just get below 200 pounds, I'd be happy," I thought to myself. I had just started my weight-loss journey, and I didn't really know what my goal should be. All I knew was that I wanted to lose weight. I was currently 225 pounds, and I remembered having been around 190 when I became pregnant with both of my children. That wasn't so bad I thought. Surely, if I can lose just 26 pounds, I'd be satisfied with that. So I set my goal. 199 it was. I reached it. And I still wasn't happy. I knew it wasn't enough because I was only one size smaller! How could this be? I thought my life would be so different. After all, 26 pounds was a lot of weight! And besides that, no one had even noticed. Really! Not. one. person. noticed that I had lost the equivalent of a toddler! I was certainly proud of myself for my accomplishment, but I knew that I deserved to be healthy, and that God wanted me to be as well. 135 was starting to feel like the goal I needed to hit. I didn't want to admit it, though, because that would mean that I had simply been making excuses all these years. Truth be told, that's exactly what they were. I have a small skeletal frame, I'm only 5'3", and 135 is a perfectly healthy weight for me. The only problem? 135 pounds was 64 pounds away!

I again went to the Lord and asked for His help. He helped me set attainable goals, 20 pounds per stage. I would only focus on 20 pounds at a time, trusting God for the next level. He was faithful. Trying to change my lifestyle and my body without having a goal was hard, to say the least. Once I organized my plan and had my goal in mind, it was much easier to finish my marathon.

Paul frequently uses athletic language in his writings, as he explains the goal of our spiritual lives. That is, to really, truly know Jesus, our

Lord, in such a personal way as to share in His nature. As with a healthy lifestyle, and with weight management in general, our spiritual lives are also a journey. We must hold to the progress we have made in growing more like Him, never turning back, and ever drawing closer to His side. Paul was willing to give up everything, his education, his standing, his reputation, his freedom, and even his very life to obtain the "heavenly prize" of eternal life.

If we are going to be successful in our Christian lives, we must set goals for ourselves as well. How do we know how to pace ourselves in the race if we can't locate the finish line? Could you set a goal for how long you will spend time with Him each day? Maybe you could set a goal for a particular ministry with which you want to be involved. Start attending a Bible study group and see where that leads. Aimlessly trying to live a Christian life without pressing toward a goal is difficult to say the least. Christ is the goal, though. Press toward Him!

What goals could you set today?

Encouragement for Today
Proverbs 21:5 *"The plans of the diligent lead surely to abundance, but everyone who is hasty comes only to poverty."* ESV

2 Chronicles 15:7 *"But you, take courage! Do not let your hands be weak, for your work shall be rewarded."* ESV

Psalm 37:4 *"Delight yourself in the Lord, and he will give you the desires of your heart."* ESV

True, I make goals for exercise, wt loss, work etc. But I don't make spiritual goals. How about a sit down quiet time c the Lord 4 days / wk.

15

Week 1, Day 7: Sabbath Rest 1

Genesis 2:2-3 *"On the seventh day, having finished his task, God rested from all his work. And God blessed the seventh day and declared it holy, because it was the day when he rested from his work of creation."* NLT

I just didn't see how this was going to work. I had learned during my first few days of my new lifestyle that weight loss really boiled down to calories in/calories out. And I realized that the more calories I burned through activity, the greater my calorie deficit would be; therefore, that would equate to more weight loss. But I was stuck this day because there was an internal struggle occurring once again. I knew that today was my Sabbath, a day my family worshipped together and rested from our work. But I was having a major dilemma as well, trying to figure out if that meant exercise too. I mean, honestly, I had extra time on Sundays to work out, and I could really put some effort into it today! In addition, I reasoned that since I'd be spending time sitting in a pew and not up cleaning my house, there would be more calories that I wouldn't be burning that day. It was decided then, that when I returned from church, I would work out. God understood after all. He wants me to care for my body!

I went 21 days straight working out, lifting weights, and having a calorie deficit of 1000/day until I realized that something wasn't right. I was tired and sore, and I felt like I had an injury in my knee. But I kept pushing. Finally I resorted to the Internet to search out my problem. I thought I was doing well, but obviously I had gone wrong somewhere. I kept reading over and over from multiple reputable websites where I needed to rest one day a week from working out in order to give my body time to recover and get ready for another week of physical activity. My muscles needed to repair, and I needed to be rejuvenated in my mind to face the mental battle I would have that week when I felt like giving up. Still not convinced that it was worth it, hesitantly I gave in to rest from workouts one day a week. To my amazement, that one day was I needed to restore me to my best.

God Himself rested. From the beginning of creation, He instituted a day of rest. This seven-day framework structured Israel's week, with the last day set aside as holy. It was to be different than the rest of the week. The first six days they were to work and live unto Him, but on the seventh day, they were to cease from their labors and worship Him.

In today's society, we want to be seen as productive and responsible members of society. The demands on modern life keep us busy and stressed out, and we need every minute possible to accomplish as much as possible. But God didn't design us in this way. He created us for work, but He also created us for rest. He even gave us time to rest! I find it amazing that a calendar week correlates perfectly with the way our bodies were designed.

I myself have chosen Sunday as my rest day. It's a day of ministry for my family, which actually keeps us too busy to do much else anyway. Our day to rest from our jobs and other work comes another day during the week. Whatever day works out best to cease workouts is fine, but ensure that you're taking that time to restore and rejuvenate your mind, body, and soul. You were designed for it!

Take some time and read the creation story as revealed in Genesis chapters 1-2. Soak in the refreshing knowledge that God has handcrafted us in His image.

Encouragement for Today
Exodus 23:11 *"but let the land rest and lie fallow during the seventh year. Then let the poor among you harvest any volunteer crop that may come up. Leave the rest for the animals to eat. The same applies to your vineyards and olive groves."* NLT

Psalm 127:2 *"It is useless for you to work so hard from early morning until late at night, anxiously working for food to eat; for God gives rest to his loved ones."* NLT

I have too many "Rest days" in my week.

Week 2, Day 1: Temptation

1 Corinthians 10:13 *"But remember that the temptations that come into your life are no different from what others experience. And God is faithful. He will keep the temptation from becoming so strong that you can't stand up against it. When you are tempted, he will show you a way out so that you will not give in to it."* NLT

"Satan just sent pizza to tempt me," my friend texted me. Someone sent pizza to her work out of the blue around lunch time, and it was smelling really good. I was glad she texted me, giving me an opportunity to encourage her and pray for her. She told me that she had brought her lunch that day, so at least she was prepared with a healthier option. I prayed for her and waited a few minutes. I was just about to text her back, asking how things were going, when she texted me back saying, "I resisted! Thanks be to God. And my friend resisted too. We ate our healthy lunches and did not cave."

Paul is writing to the Corinthian church in this chapter, giving them lessons from Israel's idolatry. Even though they were God's chosen people and had been blessed by His presence and provision, they had disobeyed and had experienced His judgment. Paul encourages them, telling them that the temptations to sin are no greater than anyone else's. There are others who have stood strong and have resisted. Furthermore, Paul tells them that God is faithful and will not allow them to be tempted beyond their capability to resist. He will always provide a way of escape, the Scripture says.

Temptation is so tricky, and it meets us everywhere, and when we least expect it. Usually, the temptation is harder to fight when we're not prepared with a way of escape. When we're hungry or tired and it seems like there's no other option, we're more likely to give into temptation. Satan's lurking around when we're alone and he whispers that it's okay. One splurge meal won't kill you. After all, millions of other people do this every day!

Oh, but no! God has provided a better way, and He's provided a way to escape temptation. In verse 14, Paul goes onto say, "Flee from the worship of idols." If we resist temptation and flee from it, we have escaped!

For me, I purposely try to avoid anywhere there might be a temptation that's strong for me. I don't go to the food court at the mall for lunch because the ratio of unhealthy options/healthy options isn't good. I eat before I leave to shop or I pick up a healthy meal somewhere else. I don't go to buffet restaurants, and I don't hang out at the ice cream parlor.

Most of all, I pray. I pray for the Holy Spirit to rescue me from my inward thoughts and I quote Scripture verses such as our key verse today. If I listen to Him, He delivers me. If I listen to the lies of Satan, I give in. The feeling afterwards is the true motivator. Will I be happier/more satisfied/closer to my goal after I eat this?

Temptation also plagues us in our spiritual lives. Giving into sin is no small thing in God's eyes. Because sin separates us from Him. God takes sin seriously and so should we. Furthermore, James Chapter 1 tells us that temptation leads to death!

Where are you struggling with temptation? Does your work environment drag you down? Try bringing your lunch and snacks and water for the day and don't visit the break room! Are you tired when you're most tempted? Make a plan for when those times occur. Think of healthy snack ideas and meals that you can prepare quickly so that you're more inclined to follow through.

Resist temptation, ask the Holy Spirit for help, and He will help you!

Encouragement for Today
James 1:13-15 *"When tempted, no one should say, "God is tempting me." For God cannot be tempted by evil, nor does he tempt anyone; but each one is tempted when, by his own evil desire, he is dragged away and enticed. Then, after desire has conceived, it gives birth to sin; and sin, when it is full-grown, gives birth to death."* NIV

Luke 22:40 *"On reaching the place, he said to them, "Pray that you will not fall into temptation."* NIV

Matthew 6:13 *"And lead us not into temptation, but deliver us from the evil one."* NIV

Read this 2 days in a row + yes, I resisted the temptation to eat chocolate. I'll treat choc as a reward so to not feel totally deprived of it.

Week 2, Day 2: Failure

Proverbs 24:16 *"The godly may trip seven times, but they will get up again. But one disaster is enough to overthrow the wicked."* NLT

Everything I've ever been good at, I've had to work extremely hard to conquer. I'm a failure. It's true. I've failed at it all. I wish that my failures had been great learning moments. I wish they hadn't been so sloppy, so ugly, so dramatic, but the truth is, I didn't take failure very graciously. When I fail, I fall hard...very hard. Anger, tears, and frustration blow up and threaten to blow away any poor soul that happens to be in my path at that moment.

That's why the first day I tried to ride my bicycle on the bike trail was so hard. For starters, it was at the end of June, and it was hot. Strike one. Secondly, there was a little incline coming back. Strike two. Going down it was a breeze, literally, going down hills on a bike is glorious! It's the coming back up part that stinks. My family had been riding a whole 15 minutes when we decided to turn around and go back to the house. Everything was going okay. I was determined to make it, marking 30 minutes of bike riding down on my activity log. And then I saw the incline (not even really a hill) looming before me. Already sweating, drops trickled in my eyes, and it stung. My legs were like rubber bands, gasping for air, I was determined that I would. not. quit. It wasn't going to happen. I was *going* to make it up this hill, and I would be victorious. Half the battle was mental, right? And I was going. to. make. it. But I didn't make it. I was about 3/4 of the way up when the nausea took over, and it was out of my control. Strike three. There was nothing I could do. I sat there on the side of the bike trail in the tall grass, so frustrated and embarrassed. "How many people saw that," was the first thing I said to my husband when he got to where I was kneeling. He assured me that it didn't matter who saw it, but it sure mattered to me! I recovered a little, walked the rest of the way up the hill, and then rode my bike on the flat part of the road back to our house. When would my new strength take over and my weakness end? I had failed. Again.

In these few verses of Proverbs, the writer gives us a bit of wisdom. Everybody fails from time to time. What separates us from others is how we handle that failure. The godly won't allow a setback to keep them down, while the ungodly only need one difficulty to knock them out. Just like fitness, times will come in our spiritual lives that threaten to knock us down. The test is whether we will get back up and keep going. The writer of Proverbs uses "seven times" in this verse to represent the many times that a person must rebound from difficulties in life. Times like these will come, be sure of that, but we must keep pressing on.

Have you failed yet? I'm sorry to put that question so bluntly, but be sure that it's going to happen. I'm not saying to go looking for failure, but don't be so hard on yourself when it does happen. Embrace the experience, learn all you can, and get back up.

Encouragement for Today
Psalm 73:26 *"My health may fail, and my spirit may grow weak, but God remains the strength of my heart; he is mine forever."* NLT

Romans 8:28 *"And we know that God causes everything to work together for the good of those who love God and are called according to his purpose for them."* NLT

Yes, I could feel so weak + defeated when my weight remains the same after weeks of trying. But it is not the end of the world. I will keep trying.

Week 2, Day 3: Your Body is a Temple

1 Corinthians 6:19-20 *"Or do you not know that your body is a temple of the Holy Spirit who is in you, whom you have from God, and that you are not your own? For you have been bought with a price: therefore glorify God in your body."* NASB

I convinced myself that it was genetic. I was overweight because generations before me were overweight. We were also from the south, and food wasn't food until it was fried. I had always been a chunky-kid. The excuses piled. I was okay. I honored God with my service, with my words, with my attitude, and with my heart, and I certainly didn't have sexual relations outside of my marriage vows. I was okay, I convinced myself. But deep inside, I knew.

In this letter to the Corinthians, Paul is addressing the problem the Corinthian church is facing in their culture regarding sexual sins. He makes it clear to them that these sins are not part of holy living in Christ. As Spirit-filled people, our bodies are a sanctuary of the living God, having been "cleansed" (v. 11).

I convinced myself in my years of Bible study that these verses only dealt with sexual sin, and I breathed a sigh of relief...I was good in that department. But my physical body as a whole certainly didn't honor God. At 5'4", weighing 225 pounds, I certainly wasn't honoring God in using my body to burn the energy that my calorie-laden diet provided.

I wanted to honor God. How could I, having been bought with a price, His own blood, do any less? After all, didn't my body belong to God? So, on June 10, I turned my body over to Him. I asked for his help, knowing that He wanted me to be healthy even more than I. I asked Him to put a hedge around me, knowing that temptation and years of unhealthy choices would bombard me at my weakest. The greatest thing about my prayer was that He answered! He heard my cry, and I committed that with His help, I would change my unhealthy habits. He and I together would provide a healthier home for my entire family. Over the next year, God provided a way of escape every single time I was tempted to give in to an unhealthy choice. To this very day, as I try to maintain my weight and honor God with my new body, He still answers, whispering to me that He has provided a better way.

Are you struggling to break the cycle of years of bad habits and unhealthy choices? Are you stuck in a busy schedule that doesn't allow time to focus on exercise and meal preparations? Ask Him for help! He will answer!

Encouragement for Today
Psalm 86:7 *"In the day of my trouble, I shall call upon You, for You will answer me."* NASB

Jeremiah 33:3 *"Call to Me and I will answer you, and I will tell you great and mighty things, which you do not know."* NASB

1 Corinthians 10:13 *"No temptation has overtaken you but such is as common to man; and God is faithful, who will not allow you to be tempted beyond what you are able, but with the temptation, He will provide the way of escape also, so that you will be able to endure it."* NASB

Take a few moments and read the entire chapter of 1 Corinthians 10. Lean in to Him. In what ways can you honor God with your body?

If I feel good about my body, I won't be obsessed with it. I can use that energy elsewhere!

Week 2, Day 4: Friendship

Proverbs 17:17 *"A friend is always loyal, and a brother is born to help in time of need."* NLT

It was time for our weekly lunch date. My two friends and I met up for lunch once a week to chat, and today was the day. It was the first time though that I would be eating food in accordance with my new lifestyle. I thought about the menu in my head, planning out what I would order, but I was afraid. I was afraid because maybe I would cave to temptation once I smelled the Mexican cuisine. I was also thinking about how my apparent lack of participation in the chips/salsa would make someone else feel. Hoping they would not feel compelled to adopt my decision, I headed in the door of the restaurant. I was first, so I sat down at the table to hostess assigned. Then the waiter came with the chips/salsa. Ahhhh!!!! My friends weren't here yet, and here I was seated at a table alone with these chips. The salsa wasn't bad, but who eats salsa without chips?

Just then, thankfully my friends arrived and we started talking about our day and what was going on in our lives. Then we placed our order. Mine was, "Three hard chicken tacos with no cheese." No cheese? I could see the confusion on their faces. Usually I ordered a chimichanga (which is fried) smothered in cheese sauce with plenty of rice, beans, and guacamole on the side. This was an apparent switch, and I really was just hoping that I wasn't making them uncomfortable. Each of us had been down this road before.

When I explained my decision and what I was doing, they were both super supportive and committed to help and pray for me. And they did. Throughout my journey, I can honestly say that all I've ever gotten from them was support.

In our text today, it is written that true friends don't turn their backs on one another in times of need. They don't make fun of one another and don't try to tear you down. They build one another up and encourage one another to be the best that they can be. Trust, support, and prayer are the main things that build friendships.

There were people at work that I called "friends" yet they taunted me every chance they could get. But these two at this table, were my true friends. I trusted them to pour my heart out, expressing the point of where I was, and I was confident they would support me, even though it may have made for some weird lunch dates. Last but

24

not least, prayer was always key. At any moment, and at any point, we still don't hesitate to ask for prayer when we're in need. And there's confidence there that the prayer happens. If you're not finding those things in your friendships, perhaps you should examine closely the value of those relationships in your life.

Who are your friends? What characteristics make the relationship strong? How did the relationship build? Hopefully there's someone in your circle you can trust, find support, and share prayer.

Take some time today and read through Proverbs 17-18 and the verses below. You will find great wisdom in those pages. Just heed it!

Encouragement for Today
Proverbs 18:24 *"There are friends who destroy each other, but a real friend sticks closer than a brother."* NLT

Job 16:20-21 *"My intercessor is my friend as my eyes pour out tears to God; on behalf of a man he pleads with God as a man pleads for his friend."* NIV

Proverbs 22:24-25 *"Do not make friends with a hot-tempered man, do not associate with one easily angered, or you may learn his ways and get yourself ensnared."* NIV

Yes, I have a circle of
friends. A few will
say "why are you on
a diet regime" + think
I don't need to loose,
but others are very
kind + √

Week 2, Day 5: Satisfaction

Psalm 107: 6-9 *"Lord, help!" they cried in their trouble, and he rescued them from their distress. He led them straight to safety, to a city where they could live. Let them praise the Lord for his great love and for the wonderful things he has done for them. For he satisfies the thirsty and fills the hungry with good things."* NLT

Every day was cause for celebration, and everyday was cause for grief. One would think that were true if they knew my eating habits before. Judging by what I consumed, I was either celebrating or grieving...every. single. day. I ate when I was glad, sad, mad, proud, angry, hurt, happy, and bored. Bored. Most of it was boredom. Some of it was recreation. Parts of it was just to draw the problems away by distracting myself with food. I have eaten to the point of pain on several occasions, and I never could get a handle on it. Another problem is that I'm a pretty decent cook and prided myself on making true southern dishes from scratch. Biscuits, gravy, chicken and dumplings, fried pork chops, fried squash, homemade mashed potatoes, and if I happened to be tired one night...fried bologna. You get the idea. Not only was the food unhealthy, but the portions were bad too. What's more, I would even eat stuff that I didn't even like. I don't like chocolate, yet, on the very day that I realized that I had to change, I was eating a chocolate bar.

I hope all of this hasn't made you hungry but see the common thread here. Self-destruction seemed to be my end game. From the outside looking in, others saw a strong independent woman that served God. Parts of that statement were true. I am strong, independent, and I served God, but there's more to my story. Way more. Inside I was a scared, frightened, embarrassed, lonely little girl that had been rejected by far too many people that claimed to love God too. They didn't like me, and quite honestly, I didn't like me either.

Like the Psalmist here, *I* cried to the Lord in true distress. He alone would have to help *me*. "Lord, help!" *I* cried too. And like Israel, He rescued *me*. He led *me* to safety. What I had always classified as a physical problem was actually a spiritual one. The physical aspect of *my* life was just a symptom of what was really going on spiritually. I felt that if other Christians couldn't love me, then I must be unlovable, and therefore, God must not take much stock in me either. I wouldn't have admitted it to anyone, but in my despair, that's how I truly felt. I was unlovable. Even in my service to Him, I always felt that I had to apologize to certain groups just because of my calling and my gender. It was only when *I* allowed God to take *total* control of *my* life that He satisfied *my* thirst and filled *me* with good things...both spiritually and physically. *I* no longer turn to food for comfort. I turn to Him. He has truly delivered me from my distress. And *I* will praise the Lord for His great love and the wonderful things He has done for *me.*

When we turn to anything or anyone else other than God for comfort and fulfillment, we will always come up empty. And when we turn to anyone or anything other than God to soothe our souls and find satisfaction, we will only find death and destruction.

As I do my best to live a healthy life, I remind myself that it is only in Christ that I will find true satisfaction. Cravings are hard. But God is good. When I'm hungry, I eat healthy food. When I'm bored, I read His word. When I feel rejected by other people, I turn to the one who always accepts me.

What about *you*? Where do *you* turn for comfort and satisfaction? Do *you* separate your physical life from *your* spiritual relationship with God? He created our bodies, and He loves *us* extravagantly. Let Him fill *you* with good things!

Encouragement for Today
John 6:35 *"Jesus replied, 'I am the bread of life. Whoever comes to me will never be hungry again. Whoever believes in me will never be thirsty."* NLT

I snack out of boredom sometimes. But I also snack out of fear! Yes, I somehow fear being hungry. I get a headache if I don't eat. What I need to do is snack on veggies instead of fruit + chips.

27

Week 2, Day 6: Physical Strength

Isaiah 40:28-30 *"Have you never heard or understood? Don't you know that the LORD is the everlasting God, the Creator of all the earth? He never grows faint or weary. No one can measure the depths of his understanding. He gives power to those who are tired and worn out; he offers strength to the weak. Even youths will become exhausted, and young men will give up. But those who wait on the LORD will find new strength. They will fly high on wings like eagles. They will run and not grow weary. They will walk and not faint."* NLT

The past few weeks had been rejuvenating as I had started my new healthy life. Finally I was starting to get into a routine, and exercising was no longer a discipline. It was something I looked forward to. I started to see myself as a runner, maybe even running my first 5k in a few months. So I went online and looked at several plans to help me learn to start running.

I have a birth defect with my eyes that has prevented me from participating in any kind of sport that involved a ball rolling, bouncing, or flying, and therefore, for the most part, I had never run...unless something was after me. So I printed off a few plans, confident that I too could become a runner.

The plans said to start out walking for 2 minutes, jogging for 1 minute, and to repeat this pattern 8 times. Well that sounded easy enough. I laced up my shoes, put my hair up, and out the door I went. I even had a snazzy little pulseometer strapped to my wrist. This was going to be fun! I walked 2 minutes, and them, bam! I shot off like a canon. I could just see the wind whipping my ponytail and just *knew* that I looked like those fit, tan college girls in my neighborhood running down the sidewalk. I mean, come on, I even had ear buds! I felt this way for a good 30 seconds! Then I realized that I was just an overweight 33 year old sweaty woman that was causing herself to develop shin splints.

I couldn't even finish the first pattern. And I had to do this 8 times! And I was only on the first day! I continued on though, determined that I could conquer this. I ended up walking 18 minutes and jogging for a combined total of 2. Exasperated, discouraged, and with lungs and legs burning, I went home, asking God all the way, "Why can't I do this?" This running plan was supposed to be for people who've never run before. And I'm not even as good as the average couch potato!

In our key verses today, Israel has faced exile, but Isaiah is prophesying to them hope, comfort, and restoration. Throughout chapter 40, we read of God's glorious power and majesty, knowing full well that creation is held in His hand. What are the oceans and mountains compared to our God? He is so great and mighty yet he loves us, his creation. Israel has been weak and disobedient, but now, they will be made strong if they trust in Him. He will renew their strength, and they will become what God created them to be.

Transformation doesn't happen overnight. There is a growth process that has to take place. When we are born again, we don't become mature Christians that very day. As His Holy Spirit takes residence in our heart, and we lean on His Word, He brings about change and healing.

Likewise, in our physical bodies, we aren't going to be strong the first day. Growth (and shrinking) has to happen. Every day that we work at it, with His help, we get closer to being the physical person that God created us to be.

Take some time today and read through Isaiah 40. See the majesty and splendor of our King. Marvel at how great He is, yet how much He loves us. Make a list of all the things God does for Israel in this chapter, and then list the things you would like God to do for you.

Encouragement for Today
Philippians 4:13 *"For I can do everything with the help of Christ who gives me the strength I need."* NLT

3 John 1:2 *"Dear friend, I pray that you may enjoy good health and that all may go well with you, even as your soul is getting along well."* NLT

Isaiah 41:10 *"Don't be afraid for I am with you. Don't be discouraged, for I am your God. I will strengthen you and help you. I will hold you up with my victorious right hand."* NLT

Week 2, Day 7: Sabbath Rest 2

1 Samuel 3:9-10 *"So he said to Samuel, 'Go and lie down again, and if someone calls again, say, 'Speak, Lord, your servant is listening.'' So Samuel went back to bed. And the Lord came and called as before, 'Samuel! Samuel!' And Samuel replied, 'Speak, your servant is listening.'"* NLT

My favorite time of the day with my family is when we have family devotion at night. We gather on our bed and read Scripture, discuss prayer requests, and then we each take turns praying for one another. The only problem is that our timing is usually late, and my husband gets up at 4:00 a.m. After family devotion, we all go to bed, and that's when my mind starts racing.

I suddenly think of all the things I haven't told my husband. Did you get your W-2 yet? The ice maker on the fridge went out, and we only have a few weeks left in our warranty. Our homeowner's insurance went up 20% this year. However, he's hovering somewhere between snoozing and REM sleep already. He doesn't hear me, and to be honest, he doesn't really care at that moment. I however and wide awake talking to thin air. Sigh. I'll have to remember to tell him tomorrow.

It seems as though when I crawl into bed at night, that's when everything important comes to the forefront of my mind. It's amazing to me how much prayer time I can get in when it's just me and God alone. The moment I grow still, that's when He speaks. He's faithful to come and meet me. Every morning when I quiet my soul with my Bible, He's always there, ready and waiting to meet me.

In the first few chapters of the book of Samuel, we read about how his mother yearned for a child. She was barren, and her hopes of having a child were looking slimmer and slimmer. Finally, Samuel is born and Hannah dedicates him to God, and Samuel actually grows up serving the Lord at the Tabernacle. One night, Samuel lies down to go to sleep but thinks he's hearing Eli calling him. Three times Samuel runs to Eli to see what he wanted. The third time, Eli realizes that God is calling Samuel and instructs him how to answer. One of the most repeated prayers for me in the Bible is this very phrase, "Speak, Lord, for your servant is listening."

It was only when Samuel was still and quiet that God came to him. This was a very dark and quiet time for Israel, as God wasn't speaking through the prophets or priests. The fact that God chose to speak to Samuel, a little boy, speaks volumes to the faith that God had in Samuel. The message to be delivered back to Eli was hard, but Samuel was brave and repeated what God had told him. From that day on, Samuel was used of God in a mighty way. Samuel had an outstanding ministry and was used mightily of God for the rest of his life. The thing that most captures my attention, though, is Samuel had to get still to hear God's voice.

In our hurried, rushed world, we have all kinds of things that crowd our minds and scream for our attention. We can get so focused on our to-do lists and personal agendas that God's voice is all but lost in the craziness of our lives. It's only when we get still and quiet that we can hear God's voice.

On this Sabbath rest day, how still and quiet are you willing to get? Can you steal some time away alone to just be with him? Don't wait until you lay down at night to tell him all the things on your heart. He wants to listen. He's interested, and he never sleeps.

Encouragement for Today
Exodus 33:14 *"The Lord replied, 'I will personally go with you, Moses, and I will give you rest--everything will be fine for you.'"* NLT

Psalm 46:10 *"Be still and know that I am God! I will be honored by every nation. I will be honored throughout the world."* NLT

It is hard to de-clutter my mind, but am trying.

Week 3, Day 1: It's Too Expensive

Matthew 25:14-30

Matthew 25:29 *To those who use well what they are given, even more will be given, and they will have an abundance. But from those who do nothing, even what little they have will be taken away.* NLT

My co-worker was exasperated. She had just gone to the grocery store and was shocked at the price of fresh produce. She had recently become interested in a life-style change but was frustrated quickly after her first grocery shopping trip. "I can't believe how much it costs to feed my family a healthy diet for just a week! My bill this week was 30% more than I normally spend, and I just don't have that every week," she said. She was discouraged. Desperately wanting to model better habits for her children, she had committed but was worried she just couldn't keep it up.

Many people blame their poor food choices on the opinion that eating healthy just costs more. In reality, this isn't always the case. Need a quick snack? A candy bar costs roughly $1.29 versus $0.50 for a lunchbox apple. Didn't have time for breakfast? Forget the $3.00 you would normally spend at the donut shop and opt for a $2.25 bowl of steel-cut oatmeal at Starbucks. For dinner, try using ground turkey instead of ground beef and save $1.00/pound, as well as about 50 calories and several fat grams per serving.

There are also other factors to consider when changing your eating habits. Eating at home is always healthier and certainly saves on the pocketbook over dining out. As you lose weight and gain muscle, clothing choices will explode and the price tag gets smaller! As you become healthier, doctor bills come less often and premiums for health and life insurance decrease. When looking at the bottom line, it all comes down to looking at the return on your investment.

Matthew's Gospel records the Parable of the Three Servants who were entrusted with their master's money. Two of the servants invested the money entrusted to them, and one dug a hole and just hid the money in the ground. In the end, the first two servants doubled their's while the third merely held onto his initial endowment. The Master was quite pleased with the first two servants, but threw out the third servant, angry that the servant didn't even make an attempt.

God has given us gifts, in today's case, our physical bodies to care for and nourish. When we fill them with unhealthy food, chemicals, and processed substances, we have not profitably invested in the body that God, our Creator, has entrusted to us. We will not see a profitable return on our investment if we continue to make unhealthy food decisions and refuse to burn the energy that our food provides. Like the master in the parable, our Master expects us to use our body to glorify Him, and that takes an investment. Remember also, not only has He created us, He has purchased us with His blood.

How will you invest? Investing the time and treasure to living a more pleasing lifestyle to honor God with our body will ultimately pay off in the end. The investment in the temple that God has created you to be will earn great rewards.

Spend a few moments today reading the entire parable (Matthew 25:14-30). Ask Him how you can better invest with what He's given you.

Encouragement for Today:
Proverbs 28:26 *Those who trust their own insight are foolish, but anyone who walks in wisdom is safe.* NLT

Proverbs 21:20 *In the house of the wise are stores of choice food and oil, but a foolish man devours all he has.* NIV

Proverbs 21:5 *Good planning and hard work lead to prosperity, but hasty shortcuts lead to poverty.* NLT

I think I do a good job at not buying junk food etc. Can't think of ways to improve at this moment.

Week 3, Day 2: Accountability

James 5:16 *"Confess your sins to each other and pray for each other so that you may be healed. The earnest prayer of a righteous person has great power and wonderful results."* NLT

As a natural introvert, it's difficult for me to ask for help when I really need it. I'm much the loner and prefer to do most things by myself. I prefer to shop alone, relax alone, and work out alone. My children know that when mommy's working out, run! But there are times when I really *need* someone there, and in those times, it's difficult for me to reach out. Reaching out, in and of itself, is out of my comfort zone. I really don't know why that is. I'm independent, strong, and I'm ashamed to say it, but I have taken great pride in those things. It's sinful, but God is working on it.

In James's letter, he writes to Jewish Christians that have been scattered abroad due to persecution. Tremendous hardships have come their way, but James offers hope and encouragement as well as instruction for Godly living. In these ending verses of the book, James encourages them to confide in one another and to pray for one another. It's incredible how much more two people together can bear than just two people individually. James knows that and instructs us to help one another.

It's Biblical to confess our sins to one another but then to also pray for one another. I'm not suggesting for a moment that we stand on the street corner and yell out all of the terrible ways we have failed God. But I am suggesting that we find trusted friends who are looking in the same direction for their lives...looking to Christ. When we find those rare people, we can build one another up, hold one another accountable, and best of all, pray for one another. James goes further in this verse, though..."that you may be healed."

Sin is a disease. Sickness happens. And unhealthy living affects our health, both physically and spiritually. We need healing in areas of our lives that maybe we haven't thought of before.

I have long held that I needed an accountability partner for my spiritual life, though, having one for my health was scary. The thought of having to confess to someone else all that I eaten and the lack of exercise that might occur was totally out of my comfort zone and altogether terrifying. Opening up that part of my life that had always been so vulnerable was going to be a tremendous hurdle.

But I did it. And it worked.

It was amazing to me to freedom I felt and the pressure that was relieved once I was able to share the load. And I shared in theirs. We encouraged one another, gently corrected one another, but best of all, we prayed for one another. Together, we were able to stand against unhealthy living.

Do you have an accountability partner? Support systems to hold you up you are important, but when you have someone that's working towards the same goal, it's so much more encouraging. Knowing that we are not alone gives us hope.

Encouragement for Today
1 Thessalonians 5:11 *"So encourage each other and build each other up just as you are already doing."* NLT

Mary + I are on this path together & it is working so far. Also in the group of Janies although contact is not established yet c̄ each gal. Need Sara's phone #

Week 3, Day 3: Time-Crunched

Ephesians 5:15-17 *"So be careful how you live. Don't live like fools, but like those who are wise. Make the most of every opportunity in these evil days. Don't act thoughtlessly, but understand what the lord wants you to do."* NLT

"People do what they want to do," my daddy always said. If I heard it once, I heard it a hundred times. And as I've grown, I realize that he is all too correct. For years, I made the excuse that I couldn't exercise regularly because I just didn't have enough time. I homeschool my children, I also work in the evenings, for years we pastored churches, and I have a home to clean, bills to pay, groceries to buy, meals to cook, errands to run.... But it's funny that I always had time for television, and the internet, and Facebook, and going shopping and to movies. In fact, I could always make time for recreation when the opportunity arose.

While I do live a legitimately busy life, I've always been able, somehow, to make time for the things I want to do. My daddy's quote is all too true. People do what they want to do. If people want to read their Bibles and pray, they do it. If people want to skip church to sleep in, they do it. People's actions define their priorities. If you want to know where you stand in any given relationship, think of where you stand on their list of priorities.

We live in a society that screams loudly that you should put self first. We don't mind at all going to buy a new outfit, having our hair done, and getting a mani/pedi. But for some reason when it comes to our health, we often put that on the back burner and stick our heads in the sand...especially when we're younger. In my years of ministry, I've visited countless older adults in hospitals, nursing homes, and in their own homes to have them tell me that they'd wished they'd taken better care of themselves. Diabetes, heart disease, and a plethora of other health issues can be avoided if we only put forth the effort when we're younger (and keep at it when we're older) to take care of our bodies that God has created.

But we serve a God whom we put first...before even ourselves. We serve Him and love Him because He loved us first. Jesus gave His life for us, and for that, I will ever worship and serve Him. But that same God we serve created us. He created our bodies in His image. Doesn't serving Him mean caring for His creation?

In Chapter 5 of Ephesians, Paul discusses living in the Spirit and by the Spirit. Paul admonishes the Ephesians not to live like fools, for they have no understanding of Him and a life in Him. He tells them to be wise, *making the most of every opportunity.* Paul tells those in Colosse the same thing in Colossians 4:5, making it somewhat of a theme in his epistles. Could it be that Paul knew that we have a tendency to procrastinate even on things that are important?

Everyday, I am given opportunities to witness to others about what Christ has done for me, and I'm thankful for those. It gives me a chance to share His love that He has bestowed upon me, and if I allow Him, He can work through me to change those around me.

Likewise, we have opportunities to care for our bodies every day. Some days are busier than others, I know, but be honest. Is there time spent on recreation and just flat-out laziness that could be better channeled into physical activity? Could you work out while you watch television? I'll be honest; this is what I do!

If we spend time taking care of His temple, we will be in a better place to mentally and emotionally to care for our families, our ministries, and those around us. It's amazing how much more efficient I've found myself to be once I've worked out for the day. Most of all, my time with Him helps me to focus on everything else, including my health. He centers me and gives me hope and peace, knowing that with Him, I can accomplish anything.

Where could you carve out more time to give to Him, first, and to care for His creation?

Encouragement for Today
Colossians 4:5 *"Live wisely among those who are not believers, and make the most of every opportunity."* NLT

Psalm 90:12 *"Teach us to realize the brevity of life, so that we may grow in wisdom."* NLT

Matthew 6:33 *"Seek the Kingdom of God above all else, and live righteously, and he will give you everything you need."* NLT

Ouch! I am guilty of choosing leisure time over exercise a lot of the time.

Week 3, Day 4: Picky-Eater

1 Corinthians 9:27 *"I discipline my body like an athlete, training it to do what it should. Otherwise, I fear that after preaching to others I myself might be disqualified."* NLT

"I know I need to lose some weight, but I don't like all of...that," my co-worker waved her hand at my plate. This particular co-worker had watched me lose the last 20 pounds and she was getting curious. Every day, she would ask me questions, but she would always refute my answers with reasons why she couldn't do it too. Today, her excuse was that she was a picky eater. So, I asked her, "What are two fruits that you like?" She told me that she liked bananas and apples and went on to share that she ate beans and corn. I came up with a few options for her off the top of my head, but I honestly thought that she just wasn't ready.

Picky eaters will struggle in areas of nutrition when trying to lose weight. Things that picky eaters enjoy *usually* tend to be starchy and full of carbs. I also enjoyed starchy foods and I still struggle with my bread consumption. But there are always options, even for the pickiest of eaters to consume. After all, the picky eaters I know typically eat the same things over and over anyway.

When I started my weight loss journey, I read countless blogs and articles of the benefits of certain foods. I wanted to know what would help me lose weight, feel full, and add to my overall health. There are foods that I regularly consume today that I never ate before I started this journey. Without this lifestyle change and research, I never would've discovered that I like Greek yogurt, green tea, or almonds. But on the flipside, there are things that I had to learn to enjoy. I always thought that raspberries tasted like soap before, but now, they're a regular part of my diet. Avocados were only to be used for guacamole, but now I use them along with greek yogurt as a base for chicken salad and sandwich spread.

While I wouldn't necessarily call myself a picky eater, I am indeed a picky exerciser. I am physically incapable of playing most team sports because of my birth defect, and I absolutely despise pushups. I can do them if I force myself, but it's just not something I enjoy. I certainly didn't enjoy running at first either, but now is a different story. Picky eaters may find themselves having to discipline themselves to eat certain things for their health, and they may actually find that in time, they start to enjoy new foods.

Paul writes in the last part of 1 Corinthians 9 about the historic Isthmian games, an Olympic type event, held in Corinth every two years. He illustrates his point of spiritual discipline is much like athletic training. If we were to compete in an athletic event, we would prepare rigorously so as to win the prize. If we're not planning to win, why play the game, right? In the same way, strict self-discipline is required if we are to grow as believers in Him. We must press on in our Bible Study and in prayer. We must submit to obeying Christ in all things, so as to win the prize of salvation, eternal life in Christ.

Paul goes onto express his fear of being *disqualified.* He expresses his concern that after he has taught others how to obtain the prize, he might not get it himself. Therefore, he has disciplined himself in such as a way so that he would not fall away from Christ.

As we transition ourselves into living a healthy lifestyle, we often find that changes are hard. We are accustomed to living one way only to change several things at one time. Those changes may be uncomfortable, but we press on, knowing that our discipline will win us the prize in the end!

Enjoy some time today reading through 1 Corinthians 9-10 and see how Paul explained food consumption and discipline. It's quite enlightening and encouraging!

Encouragement for Today

1 Corinthians 8:8 *"It's true that we can't win God's approval by what we eat. We don't lose anything if we don't eat it, and we don't gain anything if we do."* NLT

1 Timothy 4:4-5 *"Since everything God created is good, we should not reject any of it but receive it with thanks. For we know it is made acceptable by the word of God and prayer."* NLT

Matthew 4:4 *"'People do not live by bread alone, but by every word that comes from the mouth of God.'"* NLT

Week 3, Day 5: Internal Thoughts

Philippians 4:8 *"And now, dear brothers and sisters, let me say one more thing as I close this letter. Fix your thoughts on what is true and honorable and right. Think about things that are pure and lovely and admirable. Think about things that are excellent and worthy of praise."* NLT

I'll never lose this weight. I just wasn't meant to be thin. It's genetic, and there's nothing I can do about it. I'm just not good enough. If I had more faith, this would be a breeze. I'm just a failure, and that's all there is to it. Who am I kidding? People will just think I'm trying to be something I'm not.

All of these thoughts ran through my head on a daily basis. If I'm honest, I'll admit that they still run through my head from time to time. I heard a pastor say one time, "God convicts; Satan condemns." That quote has changed my entire thinking process when it comes to myself. The bad thoughts that come to mind when I'm feeling down are only whispered to me by Satan, but I choose whether or not to believe them.

See, Satan is the author of lies. Therefore, whatever he says to us, we can be sure, is a lie. Jesus, however, speaks truth, life, love. How do we know the difference? When Jesus speaks critically in our lives, it's out of love and always offers a solution and an offer of forgiveness. When Satan speaks critically in our lives, the message is always ultimate failure and leads to depression and even death.

In this chapter of Philippians, Paul is closing his letter but offers them this encouragement. He says that if they give up worrying, pray about all things, they will experience true peace. Therefore, he says, to think about things that are good.

Our thought process drastically affects us. I believe that the trail of my thoughts affects how I make decisions, how I treat others, and ultimately, my relationship with Him. If I'm not careful, my joy is stolen, my peace is gone, and I'm filled with anxiety. But Jesus offers peace, contentment, and fulfillment. How I longed for a life with those things...in every area of my life. He brings them all! And He wants you to see yourself just as He sees you, with love.

When it comes to my physical fitness, I'm still a little awkward. I don't have as much coordination as others do; I can easily get embarrassed and frustrated. But I have to keep my focus on the purpose of my exercise. And I have to keep my focus on being as healthy as I can possibly be so that I can serve Him longer.

What are your internal thoughts about yourself? Do you see yourself as God sees you? Read the entire chapter of Philippians and remember what encouragement that Christ gives us.

Encouragement for Today
Titus 3:10 *"If anyone is causing divisions among you, give a first and a second warning. After that, have nothing more to do with that person."* NLT

2 Corinthians 10:5 *"With these weapons we break down every proud argument that keeps people from knowing God. With these weapons we conquer their rebellious ideas, and we teach them to obey Christ."* NLT

I definitely have a history of a poor self image. Always comparing myself to others, always accentuating my lackings + inadequacies instead of my positive traits. Satan does fill my mind ī half truths, enuf to keep me focsing ↓ on myself. And I must be allowing him to do that. Not good! I am made in God's image + am a desirous child of God.

Week 3, Day 6: Discipline

Hebrews 12:11 *"No discipline is enjoyable while it is happening--it's painful! But afterward there will be a peaceful harvest of right living for those who are trained in this way."* NLT

I use coupons like a mad woman. If fact, I've held a few couponing seminars to teach others the methods that have proven effective for saving my family thousands of dollars a year. Some call me a cheap skate. I call myself smart. Coupons are a wonderful way to save money, and to me, it's totally worth it. At one point, I was saving my family over $500 a month just by spending about 4 hours a week working on my strategies and plans.

But there's a catch. You can't stop. When you first start, you don't save as much because your bank of coupons/rebates have to get stocked. There's not as many coupons in your stash as when you've been collecting them for a few weeks. If you miss a week of the Sunday inserts, you've messed up, and it's sort of like starting over. Missing just one week of those precious legal counterfeit dollars is detrimental to your success. And it's crucial that you are disciplined. If you just toss them all in an envelope and race off to the store, you will find yourself in a mess. Hours have to be spent preparing your plan, making lists, and reading coupon blogs in order to see the best deals. You may save some money with this method, but you will in no way see the same results as someone who has put in the time to prepare for shopping trip.

The author of Hebrews speaks in chapter 12 of God's Loving Discipline. I was shocked to learn that there are at least eight definitions for the word "discipline." While it can be used as both a noun and a verb, the indication is that discipline is used to make us better. Leading a disciplined life, receiving discipline in the form of punishment, and disciplining ourselves to learn a new skill all point to bettering ourselves for something else to come. It's important, and the Bible speaks very clearly that discipline is a good thing, although painful. But Hebrews's author is clear. The purpose of discipline is to make us more like Him. And it brings about a *"peaceful harvest of right living."* Isn't that a beautiful term?

When we are lazy and unintentional in our spiritual lives, we need to expect the same results. Not devoting our time to prayer, Bible Study, and worship will only lead to a relationship that is stale and lacking in fervor. Where our time is spent will become the treasure of our hearts.

Likewise, healthy living requires discipline. If we are intentional in
our nutrition and exercise, we will see a healthy body. But if we are
lazy and sloppy in taking care of His Temple, we will only see
likewise results. Only exercising occasionally will not help if we are
not disciplined in our routines. Slipping in junk food also does
detriment to the good that we are trying to do when we prepare
healthy food. But the painful discipline that we adhere to will only
produce a wonderful harvest if we only persevere.

Do you need to cultivate discipline? The Scripture says that He will
help us if we seek it. The Bible also says that discipline is the mark
of a Spirit-filled life.

Encouragement for Today
Proverbs 3:11-12 *"My child, don't reject the Lord's discipline, and
don't be upset when he corrects you."* NLT

Proverbs 25:28 *"A person without self-control is like a city with
broken-down walls."* NLT

Proverbs 12:1 *"To learn, you must love discipline, it is stupid to hate
correction."* NLT

1 Corinthians 9:27a *"I discipline my body like an athlete, training it
to do what it should..."* NLT

I used to have good self-discipline + control, but am finding it harder + harder. But then, I don't pray about it either

I do like to compare myself with others who obviously do not have self control, but that doesn't help me at all. This is about me, not them. —

43

Week 3, Day 7: Sabbath Rest 3

John 15:11-12 *"I have told you these things so that you will be filled with my joy. Yes, your joy will overflow! This is my commandment: Love each other in the same way I have loved you."* NLT

During this past Christmas season, I was tasked with creating a window display for our store. Part of that display included the letters "J-O-Y," cascading down an old ladder. I bought the 9" paper mache letters and brought them home to spray paint them red. I didn't want to just lay them in the grass to paint them because I just knew that dead grass sprigs would get caught in the wet paint. So I laid them on our concrete driveway, confident that any residual paint would wash away when the winter rains/ice came in the new year.

That very day that I painted those letters, my husband came home to find "J-O-Y" outlined on the driveway. He said he knew instantly what I was doing but wished I might've used a cardboard box or something as a backdrop. I wished I had too. I was still optimistic about it eventually washing away, but to my dismay, it's still there as bold as it was the day I painted it.

But I have to say that what I once saw as something unsightly, I now see as a daily reminder. Every day when I leave for work, I see JOY, a reminder of what God has done in my life. And every day when I come home from work, I see JOY, a reminder that nothing can wash away my joy.

John records in his Gospel, the words of Christ about loving one another. Jesus states very plainly that if we simply love Him and one another, our joy will be full, *overflowing* to be exact. It's interesting to me that Jesus basically says that our joy is dependent upon how we love Him and one another, and He even uses Himself as the example. Just as Christ has love us, and gave His life for us, we are also to love one another. Our love for one another is not dependent upon how others treat us. It's dependent upon how we treat others, and how we share His love with them. And how we love Jesus...well, we must simply obey Him. How much easier could it be?

In modern times, we may sometimes confuse happiness with joy. Happiness is circumstantial, dependent upon the happenings in our lives. Joy is the knowledge of the abiding presence of God. I don't know about you, but I choose joy over happiness any day. When hard days come, and it seems like there's no end in sight, happiness fades, and washes away. Joy is still there. The assurance of knowing that He is with us is a comforting peace that supersedes anything we may be facing.

Do you have joy in your heart? The Scripture says to remain in Him, the true Vine, and He will cause you to bear fruit, His joy.

Encouragement for TodayJames 1:2-4 *"Dear brothers and sisters, when troubles come your way consider it an opportunity for great joy. For you know that when your faith is tested, your endurance has a chance to grow. So let it grow, for when your endurance is fully developed, you will be perfect and complete, needing nothing."* NLT

John 16:24 *"Ask, using my name, and you will receive, and you will have abundant joy."* NLT

I like the definition: "Joy is the knowledge of the abiding presence of God." I have to admit I go by "happiness" + not "joy." Circumstances affect my happiness + I tend to think that is it. But behind that, I should feel the strong sense of joy - to carry me through the "unhappy" times in my life. It isn't always about feelings - its knowledge + recognition of God's peace + joy.

Week 4, Day 1: Support System

Ecclesiastes 4:9 *"Two are better than one, because they have a good reward for their toil."* ESV

My husband and I vowed on March 10, 2001 to be one another's constant companion and partner for life and ministry. We prepared ourselves as much as possible for the commitment that we were going to make, but we really never could've understood it until we lived it. Since that day, we have added two children, survived 4 surgeries, wiped one another's feverish brows (and a few other things too), and ministered side by side. When I decided that I needed a life change personally, I knew that he would be on board to not only support me but to participate too. I didn't even have to ask.

We have spent the last three years working opposite schedules on most days, but knowing he was there, working toward the same goal encouraged me and pushed me forward. Knowing that when I was at work, he was busting it in his workouts, held me accountable to do the same thing when I was at home. I knew that I could trust him to hold to his end of the bargain concerning his nutrition too. See, he manages a coffee shop. Temptation greeted him every day and in every moment. Croissants, cinnamon rolls, banana bread, lemon loaf, and a plethora of sugary drinks met him every day and in every moment. But I never had to question whether he was faithful because he had always been faithful to me in everything else.

On days when I was discouraged and unmotivated, he gently encouraged me. And on days when he thought he was too tired to workout after work, he told me that seeing the evidence of my workout that morning motivated him to get up and move. When time allowed, we went on family bike rides and jogs around our neighborhood. Now, almost two years later after our home transformation, my favorite times are spent working out with him. Without his support all of this time, I never would've made it. I'm so thankful for a spouse that loves me enough to encourage me to be better and stronger.

I'm not so naive as to believe that everyone may be married to someone that's motivated too. But having someone who is working toward the same goal as you would push you so much further. Knowing that there is someone out there that's going to hold you accountable will keep you on track longer and will help you overcome temptation.

Throughout Scripture, we read that God created us for community and for companionship. In Solomon's wisdom, he states in our key verse that we are better off when we have someone else to depend on and the knowledge that they're depending on us as well. If one person falls, there is someone else there to help them get back up; however, if you fall alone, you're alone.

Having support also makes all the difference in our spiritual lives. God saw when He created Adam that he needed a helpmate and God made Eve. God created us this way for a purpose.

Who do you have in your life that may be a great support system for you and you for them? Would your spouse be willing to change things to live a healthier life? Is there someone in your extended family that would like to be more fit or active? Could there be someone in your small group or church family that needs to succeed in weight loss? Look around your circles.

Encouragement for Today
Genesis 2:19 *"Then the Lord God said, 'It is not good for the man to be alone. I will make a helper who is just right for him.'"* NLT

Proverbs 17:17 *"A friend is always loyal, and a brother is born to help in time of need."* NLT

Proverbs 27:17 *"As iron sharpens iron, a friend sharpens a friend."* NLT

Yes, Gary is also on a diet to loose wt. He doesn't allow me to say anything but seeing him record his meals Reminds me to do it also. I do try to encourage him when possible. I will try to get a "friends phone" going so to communicate more.

Week 4, Day 2: Self-Control

Galatians 5:22-23 *"But the fruit of the Spirit is love, joy, peace, patience, kindness, goodness, faithfulness, gentleness, self-control; against such things there is no law."* ESV

My sister will probably shoot me when she reads this post someday, but it's a great story to prove my devotional thought for the day. She is 3 years older than me, and my only sibling. We did everything together as children, for the most part. This particular Sunday happened to be our mother's birthday, and our dad had baked her a cake, complete with frosting. I think it was Italian Creme. Anyway, Sunday afternoons in our home were typically nap times, but my sister and I weren't sleepy. We knew that cake was just sitting under the Tupperware Cake cover in the kitchen...just sitting there. And we knew our parents were asleep. To the kitchen we tiptoed to just get a little finger swipe of that delicious icing. We stuck our little pinkies in that icing, licked it off, but then quickly realized that one little taste would definitely not be enough. The sugar was calling us back, and back we went. In fact, we went back so many times that when we stopped, there was NO icing left on that cake. We had finger-licked the entire cake clean. What were we to do? Put the Tupperware cover back on! They'll never notice! Inwardly, we both knew what would happen, but little girls can hope, right?

Paul speaks in Galatians 5 of the marks of the Holy Spirit on a person's life. These things are the evidence that the Holy Spirit dwells in you and lives through you. When He takes up residence, the evidence that He is there are things like love, joy, peace, patience, kindness, goodness, faithfulness, gentleness, and *self control*. An entire sermon series and even a college course could be taught on these two verses alone, but today, I'd like to just focus on the self-control part.

Paul emphasizes here that because we are saved and filled with His Spirit, we no longer need to live life by our own strength but by His Spirit. He gives us the power to produce the kind of fruit referenced here in this verse. Self-Control. Self-control is something that I've struggled with my entire life. I've lived a moral life, never stealing, never murdering, never vengeful and spiteful, but I definitely have self-indulged. I've indulged in hurling hurtful words to make myself feel better, telling lies when it benefitted me, and eating so much that I went into an emotional coma just to drown my sorrows.

48

Overall, I've always battled with self-control. Living a self-controlled life, though, is something that marks us as Holy-Spirit filled people. I want to share His love, joy, and peace with others, along with every other good fruit He produces, but I can't just leave out self-control. What catastrophes we would make of relationships and situations if we didn't exercise self-control! And imagine what catastrophes we could avoid if we did.

The great thing here about this list isn't the gifts we receive when He fills us though, it's the fact that He _gives_ us the power to control ourselves! Don't you see? He tells us to be _self_-controlled, but He empowers it! How awesome is that?!? We don't have to live life realizing only after we've licked the frosting off the entire cake that we should've done better.

Where do you need to exercise self-control? Is it in your nutrition, exercise, or speech? Ask Him to help you. He gives us the power to live life pleasing to Him.

Encouragement for Today
Proverbs 25:28 _"A person without self-control is like a city with broken-down walls."_ NLT

2 Peter 1:5-7 _"...make every effort to respond to God's promises. Supplement your faith with a generous provision of moral excellence, and moral excellence with knowledge, and knowledge with self-control, and self-control with patient endurance, and patient endurance with godliness and godliness with brotherly affection, and brotherly affection with love for everyone."_ NLT

2 Timothy 1:7 _"For God has not given us a spirit of fear and timidity, but of power, love, and self-discipline."_ NLT

I need self control with my portions, with snacks. Self discipline to Record what I eat.

Isn't it amazing! He gives us the power to be self controlled

Week 4, Day 3: Eating Out

Proverbs 23:1-3 *"While dining with a ruler, pay attention to what is put before you. If you are a big eater, put a knife to your throat; don't desire all the delicacies, for he might be trying to trick you."* NLT

After a few weeks of healthy living, the point came where my family was going to have to go out to eat. I had avoided this at all costs so far, because the thought of not being able to totally control my food selection was scary to me. And what was more, I wasn't even able to control where we were going. My good friend's birthday was today, and she had invited our family to her party at a local steakhouse. I thought to myself, well, they have salads...I can just order a salad. So to the steakhouse we went. The only problem...they didn't have any meal salads...only small side ones. I ended up eating a bowl of lettuce and tomatoes with no dressing because there was no fat-free ranch! I felt like everyone was staring at me, thinking I had taken this whole weight loss thing to the extreme. I was certain they were planning my intervention right then and there. After we got home, I was able to eat a little more, meeting my nutritional needs of the day. But I was frustrated and wondered if my family would ever be able to eat out ever again. If I had just spent time doing a little research, I could've avoided the problem and had a much better time.

Our wise proverb today speaks of dining in unfamiliar territory. While this Scripture probably is referring to a young man's manners and test of self-control, this truth still applies when trying to live a healthy life. We must pay attention to what is served to us. We are not always going to be able to control the things that we eat, especially in today's society. Just because something "looks" healthy, doesn't mean it is. Condiments, sauces, and oils hide tons of calories/fat that we would otherwise not even notice. Birthday parties, family celebrations, holidays, church potlucks, and work luncheons serve to put a dent in our well-planned food choices. But we can still be faithful to eating healthy, even in all of those situations.

The main thing that helps me stay on track is paying attention to restaurants' nutritional information. More and more restaurants are posting their calories/fat/protein calculations on their menus/menu boards. Also, more restaurants realize that more people have dietary restrictions, therefore, they are attempting to meet the demand by adding more healthy options. My best advice, to be totally prepared is to try to view the entire nutritional information online before you even go to the restaurant. Have your order in mind before you go, so as to better fight temptation once you arrive and the aroma hits.

Secondly, don't be afraid to ask for substitutions. I am a people-pleaser, and I hate to inconvenience people. I hate to ask servers to specialize my meal, and I hate even worse, sending an order back. But I've learned to do it. Substituting that baked potato for grilled vegetables, or simply taking the processed cheese off of my chicken tacos has saved a TON of calories, simply by asking. Restaurants customize meals all the time...why not do it for you too?

Thirdly, my family avoids fast-food altogether...unless it's Taco Bueno or Chick-fil-A. Fast food typically is calorie/fat laden, and the sodium content is out of the roof! Taco Bueno and Chick-Fil-A have healthy options that our whole family enjoys, and they don't break the bank!

The best advice I can give someone is to simply eat at home. It's cheaper, it's honestly faster, and you know exactly what you are putting in your body. When you find yourself in a situation where you have to dine out, put some time in first doing a little research. It will pay off!

Encouragement for Today
Proverbs 17:1 *"Better a dry crust eaten in peace than a house filled with feasting--and conflict."* NLT

1 Corinthians 8:8 *"It's true that we can't win God's approval by what we eat. We don't lose anything if we don't eat it, and we don't gain anything if we do."* NLT

I don't understand that last verse. But in context, it is talking about food offered to idols & then eaten. I'm trying to ✓ the relevence to dieting - ?

Week 4, Day 4: Cravings

1 Peter 2:2-3 *"You must crave pure spiritual milk so that you can grow into the fullness of your salvation. Cry out for this nourishment as a baby cries for milk, now that you have had a taste of the Lord's kindness."* NLT

The craving was killing me, and it was all I could think about. Comfort food was what I wanted: macaroni and cheese, mashed potatoes, a fried pork chop, anything would do. Usually my cravings were triggered by my mood or by the demands of my day, and today had been hard. Where could I get comfort food? If I cooked it myself, I would have to go shop for the ingredients and then cook it. That would take too long though. The only restaurant within driving distance that served such delicacies was typically crowded on this day. But off we went. I was in search of starch, and starch I was going to get. When we arrived, the line was coming out the door, and there was a 45-minute wait to get a table. This would never do because I was convinced that any moment now, I would faint from starvation. I. was. hungry.

But then I remembered how I had prayed for God to help me every day as together we changed my lifestyle. Even that morning, I prayed for God to put a hedge of protection around me, shielding me even from myself. And He had been faithful. I, however, had not.

Cravings are difficult to withstand, even on our strongest days. But there are alternatives to curbing and satisfying our cravings. There are plenty of "eat-this, not-that" type websites out there, and one only needs to take a peek at Pinterest to see substitutions that are supposedly satisfying to most common cravings. I have used all of these ideas, and most of them do honestly work for me. But the main point that we need to remember is that we don't live for food. Food is provided to fuel our bodies. While it may not be fun to think about in a culture that builds special events around food, it's true. Food is simply fuel for our bodies.

Peter's readers were enduring great persecution. He calls them in this book to live above it, being faithful in the midst of hardships, scorn, and ridicule. In order for them to remain faithful though, they must press in to God, craving His word and His presence. Now that they have been born again, they must be fed, trust in Him that what He provides is good, even while enduring trials. Verse 3 even indicates that they know what goodness He provides because they've experienced it already. Remember the goodness of God!

Sometimes when we're faced with a difficult day or circumstances, we want to return to what's comfortable. We fool ourselves by thinking that there's something satisfying to that delicacy that we've always held in high regard. But we have now tasted the goodness of healthy living. How can we turn back now? We need to press on, trusting that our newness is worth it in the end.

How can you help curb your cravings before they start? Is it sweets, salty snacks, or comfort food? In a culture today where fitness is becoming more popular, companies have tried to roll out products designed to fill such cravings, and they are readily available. Do your homework and prepare beforehand to crave good things.

Encouragement for Today
Galatians 5:16 *"So I advise you to live according to your new life in the Holy Spirit. Then you won't be doing what your sinful nature craves."* NLT

1 John 2:16 *"For the world offers only the lust for physical pleasure, the lust for everything we see, and pride in our possessions. These are not from the Father. They are from this evil world."* NLT

Yes, I crave Cheetos, Fritos sometimes Chex. Often I feel I need carbs. I want to desire more veggies. I go to fruit first, but that is calories and yeast producing for me. I need to fix up snack bags of a mixture of veggies! Will do!

Week 4, Day 5: Triggers

Galatians 2:20 *"I myself no longer live, but Christ lives in me. So I live my life in this earthly body by trusting in the Son of God, who loved me and gave himself for me."* NLT

Rejected again. I knew that with our out-of-state move, it would prove difficult for me to find a job in the same field as before. I had worked in banking, but because I homeschooled my children, I could only work late afternoons and evenings. Moving to rural Mississippi, those kind of jobs just weren't available. We had been here a year when I finally found a job ad that I could even apply for. It was perfect...well, almost. It was in banking, and the hours were what I needed. I was slightly over-qualified, but I was confident that my experience would put me at the head of the pack. I was wrong. I didn't even get an interview. And to add insult to injury, a 20 year old man with no banking experience got the job instead of me.

When I got the reject email, I knew before even opening it. A rational person would remember that I gave this situation to the Lord, asking Him to lead me and open only the door He had for me. If I kept my eyes on Jesus, He would lead me to where I needed to be. But all I saw was rejection. This was bad for my health, and I knew it. Rejection is my trigger, both for my emotional health and my physical health. It threatens to send me into a downward spiral of depression and propels me to over-indulge, numbing my disappointment with comfort food.

"Triggers" is what I call them. They're little annoyances, happenings, and occurrences that cause us to stop working out and over-eat. They may come in different forms, some good, some bad. For me it's the feeling of rejection and sadness, and for others, it could be celebrations, the fact that weekend has arrived, or that they're hanging out with their best friend. Triggers are numerous, can be sneaky, and are as varied as the people that experience them. We just have to be aware of them and have a plan of action in place when it happens.

In this passage, Paul is encouraging Peter to live beyond the law. Christ gives freedom from the law, and He gives us power because Christ lives in us. We crucify our old selves with Christ, and we live by faith in Son of God. Jesus Christ gave Himself for us, and He did that so that we may live a life of freedom. We don't have to live life, bound by triggers, temptations, and failures. Our lives and the choices we make don't have to be dictated by circumstances or other people. We live by faith, walking in obedience to Christ. He rules and reigns, and it gives us such freedom when He does!

I am proud to say that this trigger only warranted a 3 ounce bag of caramel rice cakes. It's a much different scene than it would've been years ago. Because Jesus is our overcomer, we can allow Him to fight our battles for us. We don't have to give in or feel defeated when triggers come. Be sure, that the momentary feeling will pass, but you will be left with the consequences of your actions in the moment.

What are your triggers? The first step to overcoming is being aware of them. Take some time to make a list and a plan of action for when they come. Because they will come. Simply being aware of them will help you overcome.

Encouragement for Today
Psalm 56:3-4 *"When I am afraid, I will trust in you. In God, whose word I praise, in God I trust; I will not be afraid. What can mortal man do to me?"* NIV

John 8:32 *"Then you will know the truth, and the truth will set you free."* NIV

After journey, - "Reward" trigger
After watching grandkids "Reward trigger"
  Action: Veggies, a protein +
    a bit of carb > Rice crackers,
    yogurt & Rice cereal
when nothing is pressing, so I
  find myself in the kitchen,
  wanting to bake etc.
    Action - take out a veggie bag
      + drink some tea.
Craving for cheetos or chips —
  Eat veggies + a small
  helping of cheetos, & eating
  slowly.

Week 4, Day 6: What's On Your Plate

Genesis 1:29 *"Then God said, "Look! I have given you every seed-bearing plant throughout the earth and all the fruit trees for your food."* NLT

Genesis 9:2-3 *"All the animals of the earth, all the birds of the sky, all the small animals that scurry along the ground, and all the fish in the sea will look on you with fear and terror. I have placed them in your power. I haven given them to you for food, just as I have given you grain and vegetables."* NLT

Growing up in the deep south, it was typical for my family to have a big garden every summer. Corn, peas, green beans, tomatoes, okra, greens, squash, cucumbers, and cabbage were available to us year-round because of the canning that we did in the summer. My dad is a pastor, and it was also typical for community members to give us meat and to share in the harvest of their gardens and orchards as well. Overall, I grew up with a healthy core diet. I appreciate the variety of the foods that God created for us to enjoy, and I've always loved trying new things. Over time, though, unhealthy food choices and portions had crept their way into my life, and before I knew it, the food had overtaken me.

From the very beginning of creation, God put a food system in place for us, His most precious creation. He provided for us a way to live even before He hand-designed Adam from the dust of the ground. As society has grown, we've labeled things as good or bad, based on fad diets and societal pressures. Even within Christian circles, we've adopted certain guidelines that we feel that God would want us to follow. But the underlying truth that still remains is that God created food just for us. There were guidelines of course put in place, but those guidelines were to protect us, not to keep us from enjoying something good. They weren't meant to spoil our fun but to help us live healthy, productive lives for Him.

We can gain so much wisdom about what God desires our diets to look like simply from reading His Word. He gave us every seed-bearing plant, fruit, poultry, fish, protein, grain, and vegetables. Later on in the New Testament, the former restrictions were lifted. Nothing is off-limits.

What we have to remember is that God meant for us to have a balanced diet. Yes, I really do read that. He doesn't mean for us to live simply on starches and fat. He designed lean protein, green vegetables, and grains as well for us to consume because from those foods, we gain necessary vitamins and minerals. Every type of food contains different nutrients that our body needs, and when we leave one type out, we're cheating our bodies of all that it needs to function properly!

Often times, I think of those summer gardens and how they benefitted me. Growing up with a diverse diet helped me to appreciate all that God had created, and made the transition back to a healthy lifestyle so much easier. Today I visit farmer's markets and check my nutrition log daily to ensure that I'm hitting balanced targets of proteins, fats, and carbohydrates.

What's on your plate? Are you balancing your nutrition the way God designed it to be? Take a few moments and check up on the nutrients that you are consuming. Adjust where necessary.

Encouragement for Today
1 Timothy 4:4-5 *"Since everything God created is good, we should not reject any of it but receive it with thanks. For we know it is made acceptable by the word of God and prayer."* NLT

He even made the sugar cane plant so we can have sugar! + the chocolate bean!

I am trying to balance the diet - trying to be heavier on veggies recently.

Week 4, Day 7: Sabbath Rest 4

Mark 8:1-4 *"About this time another large crowd had gathered, and the people ran out of food again. Jesus called his disciples and told them, 'I feel sorry for these people. They have been here with me for three days, and they have nothing left to eat. If I send them home hungry, they will faint along the way. For some of them have come a long distance."* NLT

Every work day of my job began the same. I would drive to the parking lot of my building early on purpose so I would have time to pray before going in. Dread filled me with the knowledge that I would have to face him and hear him rant about how stupid I was every single day. The truth was, he treated everybody that way. There was certainly no favoritism around there. The bad thing about it was that it was a Christian environment. My co-workers and I did our best to maintain the peace and to walk on eggshells around him, but you never quite knew when he would blow. Even in our devotion time, he would use any opportunity to put us down. One time he even held a devotion on respecting authority and prayed over us that we as his employees would "know our place." He would start tapping his foot and curling his lip in an annoying way that let everyone know when he was mad. I hated it here, and there was no end to it in sight. But for some reason, God had me here, and I didn't know why. I still don't know why to be exact. But I know that every day, God gave me the grace I needed to face him, and He still gives me that same sweet strength to live the life He's given me.

One day before going into work, I searched the Scriptures for something to hold onto as I worked my shift. Mark 8 was just the nourishment I needed. Jesus is again faced with a large crowd, this time 4000 instead of 5000. Scholars say that these two instances were indeed different ones. All four gospels record the feeding of the 5000 with the 5 loaves of bread and two fish, but only Mark and Matthew record this one. At any rate, at the first feeding, the Scriptures say that Jesus had compassion because the people were like lost sheep without a shepherd. This time, however, Jesus has compassion on them simply because they were hungry. They were physically hungry, and Jesus was concerned. What's more, they were apparently in the middle of nowhere and had been so for three whole days. There was nowhere to get the food, and the disciples had apparently forgotten that they were in the presence of a miracle-worker who had done far greater miracles than this.

Nevertheless, Jesus worked through those doubting disciples to provide for the total needs, both spiritual and physical, of the entire crowd.

Now isn't that just like Jesus? He's not just concerned about our spiritual needs, although this is incredibly important. He's concerned about our every day, physical needs too. There is nothing too big for God to handle, and there is nothing too small for Him either. He cares whether or not we're nourished and healthy or whether we're lifeless and dull, burdened down with unhealthy environments or food.

As it relates to health, I think God is keenly interested in how we fuel our body, His creation, for the day. If we are truly nourished with good things, we will be better equipped to handle stressful situations, even those involving others who label themselves as a Christian.

As it relates to our spiritual life, Jesus is still the Messiah who has compassion on us and who will nourish us with His presence and His love. No matter what/who we face, we can rest with assurance that He is still the same compassionate Shepherd who feels our pain. He understands, and He cares.

Take some time today to read the entire chapter and marvel again at how good our God is and has compassion for our every day needs.

Encouragement for Today: Mark 5:43 *"Jesus gave them strict orders not to tell anyone what had happened, and then he told them to give her something to eat."* NLT

Matthew 5:3 *"God blesses those who realize their need for him, for the Kingdom of heaven is given to them."* NLT

Talked ē 2 people who have heavy issues/needs. Reveal to them that you provide ① power to resist the wrong food (Laurie) ② strength in time of grieving (Donna)

Week 5, Day 1: Eagerness

Galatians 6:7-9 *"Don't be misled--you cannot mock the justice of God. You will always harvest what you plant. Those who live only to satisfy their own sinful nature will harvest decay and death from that sinful nature. But those who live to please the Spirit will harvest everlasting life from the Spirit. So let's not get tired of doing what is good. At just the right time we will reap a harvest of blessing if we don't give up."* NLT

The commitment was there, but the eagerness...not so much. Every morning, I arose and laced up my sneakers to work out, and I completed it. But I didn't really want to. In fact, a year went by before I became fully eager to embrace my new lifestyle wholeheartedly. That's the truth. It was a year. The results, however, those I was eager to reap.

Today, if I must miss a day of working out, outside of my typical day off, I miss it. Working out has become a sort of therapy for me, working off stress, and working through things that I'm sure to face in the day ahead. I don't like missing a day because I feel out of sorts when I do.

We turn to Galatians 6 where Paul is exhorting them regarding hard work. In our culture, we believe in the American dream and that with hard work, anything is possible. The sky's the limit, and the Bible also teaches the same thing. We can truly accomplish anything with God's strength and by working for it.

Paul assures them that they will reap a harvest of exactly the thing they have planted. We don't plant apple seeds and harvest oranges. We pick the fruit of the tree we have planted. Paul further urges them to live to please the Spirit rather than simply doing whatever we wish, pleasing the flesh. When we live to please self, our harvest is decay and death. But when we live to please the Spirit, we inherit everlasting life! Paul then goes a little further by encouraging them, "Let's not get tired of doing what is good..." (v. 9).

While commitment will take us a long way, it cannot take us forever. Spiritually speaking, our love for God is what pushes us further into a deeper relationship with Him. We must grow into an eagerness to love Him, to pray to Him, and to serve Him.

As we press on in our commitment to working out and eating

healthy, at some point we're going to tired of it and get bored. The nostalgia of laziness and fat-laden food will creep back in eventually. But remember, we harvest what we plant. The day I embraced that this journey was for life, those torturous thoughts stopped. As we live healthy lifestyles in a culture that loves the unhealthy, we may be tempted too easily and fall away if we rely solely on our commitment. At some point, as growth occurs, we must become eager to embrace all that it entails.

How about you? Are you eager? Have you grown further than commitment to embrace a healthy lifestyle and all it involves? Lean on Him. He will not only help you fulfill your commitment but to fall in love with pleasing Him! And in due time, you will reap a bountiful harvest.

Encouragement for Today
2 Corinthians 8:11 *"Now you should finish what you started. Let the eagerness you showed in the beginning be matched now by your giving. Give in proportion to what you have."* NLT

Acts 17:11 *"And the people of Bereawere more open-minded than those in Thessalonica, and they listened eagerly to Paul's message. They searched the Scriptures day after day to see if Paul and Silas were teaching the truth."* NLT

I will pray for eagerness to exercise!

Week 5, Day 2: Peer Pressure

Philippians 2:13-14 *"For God is working in you, giving you the desire to obey him and the power to do what pleases him. In everything you do, stay away from complaining and arguing, so that no one can criticize you. Live clean, innocent lives as children of God, shining like bright lights in a world full of crooked and perverse people."* NLT

"I've had it," I said to myself. Why can't they just ignore it if they don't like it? I had started a new position in a different division of my company just a few months before, and it was hard. We all had desk jobs, tucked neatly into our cubicles, and everyone seemed to enjoy snacking...all day long...at their desk. Every day, something sugary greeted me at my desk. Yesterday, it was candy. Today it's a cupcake. And tomorrow...well, I've already been warned...we're all getting ice cream from the Dairy Kreme across the street. Really?!? Is that all we had to do? We had a staff meeting last week where everyone got milkshakes, and I sat there with my bottled water. I honestly didn't mind, but everyone else did. I got more than a few remarks about my beverage choice and making everyone else look bad. I started to doubt. Maybe I should've at least poured it in a cup so no one would know what I was drinking. This was getting intense, and it was all because of water! I thought we were having a meeting to discuss...well, business! Now I stood at my desk staring at that cupcake and thought for a brief second, "I should just throw it in the trash can." But then I reasoned that it would be rude. Always, wanting to please people had been my biggest downfall in life, and this time was no different. I wanted to eat the cupcake so as not to repeat the episode in the business meeting last week, but I felt like I was being set-up to fail. But then again, the cupcake did look really good, and it was my favorite flavor...red velvet.

In that moment, I had to make a decision. Was I more worried about my standards or was I going to be an example to those around me who needed to see the fruit of the Spirit in my life...in this case, kindness. The Holy Spirit whispered to me that I could accomplish both. I decided that I was going to leave the cupcake on my desk while I worked. If anyone inquired if I was going to eat it, I would politely offer it to them. If no one asked, I would just quietly take it home to my children and sincerely thank the person who left it for me.

Paul writes from his prison cell to the Philippian church. They were being persecuted, Paul was in prison himself, but he wanted to encourage them to press on. He writes this letter to strengthen them and to uphold them in their ministry to those around them. The church was doing well, but discouraged they were.

Paul assures the believers here in our key verses that God is working in them. He is bringing about a change in their lives. God would strengthen them, and help them to succeed. There were those who were trying to tear them down, but God is faithful. He even went so far as to give them the "want-to" to obey Him and to please Him. Paul goes on to exhort them to perform their ministry without complaining or arguing with one another so that "no one can criticize."

We live in a world that is just waiting to pounce on Christians the moment they step out of line. It wants to pick us apart, and point out every flaw we may have. In those times, it's tempting to give into those criticisms, but God gives us a better way! He not only strengthens and equips us to press on, He even gives us the desire to do it!

Where are you struggling? Maybe there are those who are trying to pull you astray from your healthy lifestyle. Maybe there are those who are jealous of your progress, and they are criticizing your methods. Maybe you have a great support system, but you have doubts as to whether you can keep this up for long-term. And it goes beyond a healthy physical lifestyle change too. When we make changes in our lives, it will automatically affect those around us who are used to the old you. They may push back. But we can press in to Him.

Call out to Jesus. He is there, ready and waiting to give you even the desire to press on to do what pleases Him.

Encouragement for Today
Job 5:2 *"Surely resentment destroys the fool, and jealousy kills the simple."* NLT

Galatians 1:10 *"For now I am seeking the approval of man, or of God? Or am I trying to please man? If I were still trying to please man, I would not be a servant of Christ."* ESV

Romans 12:2 *"Do not be conformed to this world, but be transformed by the renewal of your mind, that by testing, you my discern what is the will of God, what is good and acceptable and perfect."* ESV

Week 5, Day 3: Self-Pity

James 4:2-4 *"You want what you don't have, so you scheme and kill to get it. You are jealous of what others have, but you can't get it, so you fight and wage war to take it away from them. Yet you don't have what you want because you don't ask God for it. And even when you ask, you don't get it because your motives are all wrong--you want only what will give you pleasure."* NLT

"You're one of those people?!" my new acquaintance asked. She was so pretty, and I was so jealous. She sang like a songbird, and her kids all behaved perfectly in church. She was maybe a size 4 and did I mention, drop-dead gorgeous. Our families were sitting at the local deli after a kids' event at church, and I couldn't get over her plate. It was loaded with things that I deemed off-limits in my strict nutritional routine. My husband had mentioned that he was sore from our earlier workout, and she stared at me in disbelief. I wasn't sure if the disbelief was coming from the fact that I was still quite overweight or whether she hated exercise that much. I was sure it was the first reason. There's no way she was that in shape and ate like this all the time. My self-doubt was creeping up. She couldn't believe that anyone this big actually worked out. I just knew it.

Nope, I was wrong. She went on to explain her disdain for exercise in any form, and what's more, she loudly proclaimed her love of Little Debbie Fancy Cakes. You know the ones. They're pale pink with frosting that looks like lace? How in the world could someone eat Fancy Cakes and have it all together?

By the time we got home that day, I was having a full-blown pity party. "Am I going to have to count my popchips for the rest of my life," I asked as I perfectly portioned out my mid-day snack. It was sarcastic, and a bit over-dramatic, but I didn't care. I needed to comfort myself with rationalizing how people like "that" existed. It just wasn't fair. How do people get "good" genes while I'm stuck with these? There are millions of women walking around every day looking fabulous while they drink soda and scarf down burgers and fries. Here I am eating carrot sticks and drinking what seems like gallons of water for 6 whole weeks, and I've barely lost 12 pounds!

I was jealous, and I was envious. The only problem was that I really wanted to be her friend. We had so much in common, and our kids loved each other. We needed to be friends, but I had a whole lot of jealousy to work through.

64

In the text today, James confronts jealousy in very plain terms. He even goes so far as to explain the consequences of their attitudes and the reasons behind their unanswered prayers. They only want what benefits them, in the way and time it benefits them. Their motives are only to please themselves, and their attitudes are rotting their relationship with Christ. Instead of turning to Him for help, they scheme a way to get what *they* want, what gives *them* pleasure.

I was just like James's readers. I had lost sight of the reason I had changed my life. The reason for my journey in the first place was to honor Him with my body, and I was doing just that. The end of my weight-loss was not even in sight yet, but currently I was indeed doing what pleased Him, just with a bad attitude. I had to realize that the only person who had RSVP'd to my pity party was me. And Jesus certainly wasn't taking part. In fact, feeling sorry for myself was only getting in the way of my relationship with Him and where He was taking me.

When frustrations, jealousy, and doubt start to creep in, don't start blowing up balloons and hanging streamers for that pity party. Turn to Him and analyze whether you are still where God wants you to be. Look carefully at your motives. Are they prideful? Ask God to help you with the right intentions at heart. He will answer you!

Encouragement for Today

Proverbs 4:23 *"Guard your heart above all else, for it determines the course of your life."* NLT

Proverbs 14:30 *"A peaceful heart leads to a healthy body; jealousy is like cancer in the bones."* NLT

Week 5, Day 4: Patience

James 5:7-8 *"Dear brothers and sisters, be patient as you wait for the Lord's return. Consider the farmers who patiently wait for the rains to fall and in the spring. They eagerly look for the valuable harvest to ripen. You, too, must be patient. Take courage, for the coming of the Lord is near."* NLT

As the weeks had crept by, I had seen minimal change on the scale. When would it come off? I was sure by now, I would've at least lost the 12 pounds I had set as my goal during my 24-day challenge. Everybody knows that people lose more weight at the first, right? 12 pounds seemed doable, but now, on day 22, it didn't look like that scale was going to budge another 2 1/2 pounds the last two days. What was I doing wrong?

I was following an exercise routine that seemed brutal to me, someone who had never been an athlete...not ever. Careful everyday, I tried to perfectly portion out my food and to abide by a strict method of eating every 2-3 hours, and I drank more than a full gallon of water everyday! I couldn't go an hour without having to run to the bathroom. Maybe I was drinking too much water, I thought. Maybe I was eating too much? Maybe I was just meant to be fat, I reasoned. I was tired of feeling fat but desperate to understand why the scale wasn't moving down faster. Maybe the scale was broken?

Deep inside, though, I knew I just needed to be patient. I knew not to pray for patience, though. Old timers had warned me not to pray for patience, always with a chuckle. But I really needed some.

Turning to James, I found that he encouraged his readers to be patient. I knew what I was going through wasn't anywhere near in comparison to people like Job and the prophets that James mentioned later in verses 10-11, but in the moment, it sure felt like affliction. James here, though, uses the illustration of a farmer waiting for his crops to ripen. He doesn't just go sit in the field, though, and wait. There's work involved. The farmer plows the ground, plants the seed, cares for the plant, plucks out weeds, prays for rain, and after ALL OF THAT, then the harvest comes. The farmer's crops don't just shoot up out of the ground quickly. After all of their work is completed, then they wait with patience.

I've planted and tended my share of gardens in my lifetime. As a child, it was a yearly family affair. I always loved the planting and the picking part, but it was the in-between part that was the chore. As I would go down the rows, planting the seeds, I would envision those big corn stalks and snap bean plants that were sure to spring up. And then once they did, I sure did enjoy the sight of it on my dinner plate. But patiently waiting for it to appear was hard! Pulling weeds was no fun. It was hard, it was hot, and there was sweat involved. But it was necessary if we were going to have a harvest.

As we tend and care for our bodies, sometimes it seems like there's no progress happening. But there is. Sometimes the scale doesn't move, in fact, there were days when it would actually go up instead of down! Sometimes we struggle with temptation, and sometimes we even fail. But we must be patient. There is a process involved when we change courses in life, but it's worth it! It's hard, it's hot, and there's sweat involved. But we must put in the work if we will reap a harvest!

Are you struggling with patience? Allow God's word to encourage you today.

Encouragement for Today
Romans 12:12 *"Rejoice in our confident hope. Be patient in trouble, and keep on praying."* NLT

Psalm 37:7-9 *"Be still in the presence of the Lord, and wait patiently for him to act. Don't worry about evil people who prosper or fret about their wicked schemes. Stop being angry! Turn from your rage! Do not lose your temper--it only leads to harm. For the wicked will be destroyed, but those who trust in the Lord will possess the land."* NLT

Galatians 5:22-23 *"But the Holy Spirit produces this kind of fruit in our lives: love, joy, peace, patience, kindness, goodness, faithfulness, gentleness, and self-control. There is no law against these things!"* NLT

_____

_____

_____

_____

Week 5, Day 5: Cheating

James 4:17 *"Remember, it is sin to know what you ought to do and then not do it."* NLT

"When is your cheat day," someone asked me in the middle of my weight-loss journey. I didn't know what they were talking about so I inquired further. Apparently, lots of fad diets boast about the once-a-week "cheat" meal or "rewards" meal. After talking about it a little more, I decided that I would indulge. After all, I'd been at this for months, and I hadn't stepped out of line at all. I deserved it, and I had missed a whole lot of cheat meals. What would one meal hurt? So I loaded up the family, and we went out for Italian food. Chicken Scampi was on my menu for the evening, and I didn't stop until I'd had the delicious breadsticks, two of them to be exact. It was so good. But in the back of my mind, I had this nagging feeling of guilt like I'd committed adultery or something. The food was good, but I felt horrible. I couldn't even enjoy my hard earned "cheat." Over the course of my weight-loss journey, I've had a few episodes like that. The food was great, but inside, I didn't even enjoy it. And I sure didn't enjoy it the next day when I stepped on the scale and had gained 2 pounds! 2 pounds! Really?!? From one meal? There's no way I had consumed that many calories! When I looked up the nutrition, I had eaten a little over 1600 calories that meal. That was more than the calorie count I allotted for a typical day!

After several occasions just like the one described above, I realized that the struggle I felt during and after my hard-earned "rewards" meal just wasn't worth it. It took two extra days just to get back to where I was before I ate the one meal, and after having a ton of carbs or sugar, I struggled with temptation all the more. For me, I decided that cheating was too hard. There really was no reward involved.

Just like my cheat meals, James warns his readers about doing things contrary to what they know to be right. It just isn't worth it, in fact, it is sin. There's no getting around it. Sin separates us from God, and as Christians, that should be the last thing we would want. Temptation is so hard, but James gives us a way to deal with it. Earlier in this chapter, in verse 7 he says, "So humble yourselves before God. Resist the devil and he will flee from you."

Many people think that in order to battle temptation in weight loss, one must indulge but just a little. Their reasoning is that if you want a cookie, go ahead and eat the cookie so as to avoid eating two later. My suggestion is to find an alternative and turn to God. We've already established that no temptation is too great for God, and now we read in James that if we resist the devil, he will flee! I think the point just boils down to whom we want to please. Do we want to please our flesh? Or do we want to please God?

Do you indulge in cheat meals? What is the struggle like after you've indulged? Is it worth it or would you be better off living a healthy lifestyle in total completion?

Read through James 4 and find encouragement from his instructions.

Encouragement for Today
Galatians 6:7-8 *"Don't be misled--you cannot mock the justice of God. You will always harvest what you plant. Those who live only to satisfy their own sinful nature will harvest decay and death from that sinful nature. But those who live to please the Spirit will harvest everlasting life from the Spirit."* NLT

Proverbs 11:3 *"Honesty guides good people; dishonesty destroys treacherous people."* NLT

_____

_____

_____

_____

_____

_____

_____

_____

_____

Week 5, Day 6: Childhood Obesity

Proverbs 31:14-15b *"She is like a merchant's ship; she brings her food from afar. She gets up before dawn to prepare breakfast for her household..."* NLT

My daughter is truly a newer version of me. Some would call her a "mini-me," but she's taller than me, so I'm now the mini version, I guess. When our baby pictures are placed side by side, one can only tell the difference by the age of the photo. And even now, whenever she is introduced, people commonly comment on how much she looks like me. All of this is why I've had a fear from the time she was a toddler that she would grow to be like me...in every way. I could see the shape of her body as I cared for her and noticed the tendencies it had. She was gaining weight in all the places that I carried mine. What could I do to help her avoid the pitfalls of my youth and encourage her to live a healthier life?

Before we had any babies, my husband and I resolved that our kids wouldn't even know about french fries and soda. Ha! I still marvel at the ignorance of people without children! There were times when they were toddlers that there were more french fries on the floor of my car than had actually made it into their mouths.

It came to my attention one day as I was grocery shopping that I really made her choices for her when it came to nutrition. She's a child, has no job, and is honestly forced to eat whatever I bring home. She doesn't get a choice of what she consumes because she can't buy something else. As I looked in my grocery cart, I saw some healthy fruits and vegetables, but what I also saw was fatty chips, cookies, and frozen pizza. What was I feeding her? How was this helping her? While I modeled a healthy lifestyle in front of her, what I actually bought for her spoke something different. I had to do something.

I'd like to report that the transition was easy in our household and we have made a full 180 turnaround. But it wasn't, and we haven't. There were arguments, frustration, and meals spent with pouting faces, but over time, it's gotten better. There are still moments when I cave and give in, and there are still nights that are so busy that we're lucky that anybody gets dinner. Overall, though, our home is much healthier, and both my children know the importance of making healthy decisions and have come to enjoy some physical activities.

Proverbs 31 is well-known as the chapter in the Bible for which to model Christian womanhood. I strive every day to live up to the characteristics described, but all too often, I fall short. These attributes give us something to strive for, to be more like Christ has designed us to be. And to my surprise, it even speaks about what we feed our families. Children don't get a choice. They don't choose which family they are born into, and they certainly don't get to choose their genes. We are their sole care-takers and have a God-given responsibility to raise them to follow Christ and to care for their bodies. They are likely to follow the patterns we set for them as children into adulthood, and they are likely to repeat the decisions we have made for them, with their children. The cycle continues.

So what's for dinner at your house tonight? What decisions are you making for your children that they are likely to repeat? If you could design the future health of your family, what would it look like? Take some initial steps today to implement that future.

Encouragement for Today
Proverbs 22:6 *"Teach your children to choose the right path, and when they are older, they will remain upon it."* NLT

Ephesians 5:1-2 *"Follow God's example in everything you do, because you are his dear children. Live a life filled with love for others, following the example of Christ, who loved you and gave himself as a sacrifice to take away your sins. And God was pleased, because that sacrifice was like sweet perfume to him."* NLT

_____

_____

_____

_____

_____

_____

Week 5, Day 7: Sabbath Rest 5

James 3:6 *"And the tongue is a flame of fire. It is a whole world of wickedness, corrupting your entire body. it can set your whole life on fire, for it is set on fire by hell itself."* NLT

"Why did I say that," I cried to myself as I drove home that day. My boss had lit a fire under me with just one comment, and that was all it took for me to spew pent-up frustration. "Do I do anything right," I said? He looked like I had slapped him, but he quickly recovered. He went on to explain how I had to have been the person to do a task wrong because everyone else had done it correctly before. Therefore, by his reasoning, it had to be me. It wasn't me, but he wasn't budging. I honestly don't know why I felt the need to defend myself that day, but he was wrong! And he had to know it! The months of his nit-picking, in my mind, had built up such resentment in me.

As I drove home that day, I rehashed and rehashed the heated conversation in my mind. He said this. Then I said that. I can't believe he would say that! Over and over it went. When I got home, I really didn't want to talk about it. I was exhausted from the emotional turmoil, but my husband deserved an answer as to why I was in such a state. And so I told him. He said this. I said that. And I went through the whole ugly story.

I was ashamed. While nothing I said was untrue or unkind, it sure was forceful. It was loud. And I couldn't stop. I knew that I was treading on thin ice and bordering on insubordination, but I couldn't stop. Why couldn't I control my tongue?

My mouth has gotten me in more trouble that I would ever care to recount. It's got me in some harrowing situations and has been the cause of my crawling back to wounded friends with shameful apologies.

I'm so glad that James tackles this subject in his letter to Jewish Christians because I for one, need to read it. James is concerned with how they speak to one another, as it influences their relationships. He says the tongue, in a sense, acts as it own agent; however, it impacts every area of our lives. While it is one of the strongest muscles in our bodies, it's also in a way, the weakest. We're unable to control it. One gets the point when they're reading through this section that it's hopeless to even try and tame it. But it's not. James is simply painting a picture of how dangerous our speech is and how it can do more damage sometimes than physical destruction. We can't take words back. And we can't undo the damage that's been done once it occurs.

Further, our well can't have two buckets. As James says in v. 11, "Does a spring of water bubble out with both fresh water and bitter water?" We can't fix it. But the Holy Spirit can. If he lives in us, out of us can flow fresh, clean, nourishing water. We don't have to hold in the bitter water that constantly threatens to spill over. As the old saying goes, "When your cup is bumped, what spills over?"

How do you handle it when you face conflicts with others? Do others know you as a loose cannon? Do you want fresh water to freely flow from you, giving praise to God constantly?

Encouragement for Today
1 Peter 3:9 *"Don't repay evil for evil. Don't retaliate with insults when people insult you. Instead, pay them back with a blessing. That is what God has called you to do, and he will bless you for it."* NLT

Proverbs 21:23 *"Watch your tongue and keep your mouth shut, and you will stay out of trouble."* NLT

Week 6, Day 1: Stuck in a Rut

Proverbs 19:15 *"Lazy people sleep soundly, but idleness leaves them hungry."* NLT

20 minutes of biking, 5 minutes of weight training, 20 minutes of biking, 5 minutes of calisthenics, and 20 minutes of biking. This was pretty much my workout routine every day for the first few months of my weight-loss journey. I'm certainly not a person that gets bored easily, in fact, I can eat the same thing every day for weeks without getting tired of it. But after several months of the exact same workout cycle, I was starting to feel like I was stuck in a rut. This method was working for me, and I was seeing results on the scale. Why would I change what was working? I was starting to form an apathetic attitude toward my normalcy, and I didn't want that. I knew that things had to change, but change was hard once again. If I allowed my boredom to consume me, I knew I would end up quitting, and I couldn't let that happen.

The proverb quoted today is a perfect fit to how I felt. Lazy people sleep, that's for sure. They become content to rest constantly, and likewise, idle people are hungry. When we become bored with our activity, we tend to stop it all together. And for me, when I am bored, I eat. It's always amazing to me when I find the solution and my motivation in God's Word. He gives us the strength and the desire to follow through with our commitments.

In our spiritual lives, God gives us all sorts of experiences to strengthen and grow us. As we read all of the different ways He's provided for us in His Word, we can enjoy drama, comedy, poetry, romance, and adventure. It never gets old!

In my physical transformation, I knew that this rut couldn't continue, but I was at a loss for how to get out of it. Reading this very proverb though motivated me to find an answer. The book of Proverbs is known as wisdom literature, so I turned to wise counsel for help. Those who had lost large amounts of weight had a wealth of knowledge as to how to change up workouts so that I wouldn't become bored. In addition, I learned that my body actually needed this variety. Over time, our bodies become stronger and then become resistant to the same old routines. We either must increase our intensity or change things up a bit. Thankfully, I learned to embrace walking and jogging, jumping rope, and pull-ups. Every day is now different as far as my exercise goes, and it never gets old!

Are you feeling stuck in a rut? Try a new sport or activity that you've always wanted to try. Try a new machine at the gym that has seemed impossible until now. You can do it, and you might just find that you enjoy it!

Encouragement for Today
Ecclesiastes 2:24 *"So I decided there is nothing better than to enjoy food and drink and to find satisfaction in work. Then I realized that these pleasures are from the hand of God. For who can eat or enjoy anything apart from him? God gives wisdom, knowledge, and joy to those who please him. But if a sinner becomes wealthy, God takes the wealth away and gives it to those who please him, This, took, is meaningless--like chasing the wind."* NLT

Yes I am, but like her, I'm content i it. I've been off exercise as we were in Vancouver last week, but will get back on schedule this week, hopefully stay healthy as Gary isn't Right now. And then get a new routine going, maybe to include stair stepping a bit.

Week 6, Day 2: Sickness

Psalm 103:2-5 *"Praise the LORD, I tell myself, and never forget the good things he does for me. He forgives all my sins and heals all my diseases. He ransoms me from death and surrounds me with love and tender mercies. He fills my life with good things. My youth is renewed like the eagle's!"* NLT

The familiar feeling greeted me as I woke that fall morning. Sore throat, headache, ears hurting, and if I sniffed...yeah, my nose was stuffy too. Sigh. I was on a roll too. I'd been doing so well, consistently getting up to exercise every day and I was feeling awesome. That customer I encountered yesterday had been sick, and I knew it. I sanitized my hands soon after they left, but apparently my gelatinous alcohol was no match for air-borne illnesses. Today would just have to be my rest day, I decided.

I opened my computer to log my activity and my food for the day but suddenly realized that I wasn't working today, thus cutting down my calorie burn further. I also had a social engagement where I would be forced to consume more calories than was typical for dinner. I *needed* to work out, but I just didn't feel like it. Quickly, I swallowed some generic cough medicine, hoping to at least work out the achy feeling, and to my relief, it worked! After breakfast, I laced up my shoes, put up my hair, and I got to spinning on my bike inside while watching last night's episode of the Biggest Loser. My intensity wasn't what it was typically, and I didn't think I would have as much endurance, but I was still burning calories. Then the sweat came. For a moment I thought I may have a fever, but after glancing at my watch, I realized that I was just getting warmed up. This was okay, and I was doing well! I made it through the entire workout, and honestly, I felt better when it was done. The sweat was somehow cleansing and gave me a chance to help clear my sinuses.

Sickness will come periodically in life. Cold/flu season is sure to bring a little sickness, and the all-too-familiar stomach bug will rear its ugly head from time to time. The questions I typically get are, "Why are you working out when you're sick? Your body needs time to rest." Yes, it's true. When our bodies are sick, we should rest. But what should we rest from? The day I detailed above was my turning point when I realized that working out when I'm sick can actually be good for me. While I don't advise over doing exercise when your body is clearly saying stop, a small common cold should not hinder us...it should propel us. As I've gotten healthier and stronger over time, my sicknesses have literally been cut by about 75%. I don't have a spleen, and I typically get every little sickness that blows my way. But by living a healthier life, my immune system has dramatically improved.

I've been on this healthy life journey for almost two years now, and I've only had two colds during that time. I've only taken one sick day in two years too. There's no coincidence that my lifestyle affects my health, even on the small mundane levels.

As I was reading this Psalm, I couldn't help but remember that the word "Psalms" itself actually means, "Praises." Isn't that awesome? An entire book giving praise to God, our Creator! There are several things that David points out that I feel are applicable to our lesson today.

First, we praise the Lord and never forget about all He has done for us. He has done mighty things for us, reshaping and remolding us to become more like Him. Secondly, he forgives our sins AND heals our diseases. Sin itself is a disease, but we're thankful that we know the cure...salvation in Christ! Thirdly, He has snatched us from the hand of death, giving us new life. And lastly, our youth is renewed!

As we are remade both physically and spiritually, we can look to Him to sustain us. When hiccups arise such as sickness, we can trust that He made our bodies, and He's perfectly capable of fixing them.

Encouragement for Today
3 John 1:2 *"Dear friend, 'I hope all is well with you and hat you are as healthy in body as you are strong in spirit.'"* NLT

Romans 5:3-4 *"We can rejoice, too, when we run into problems and trials, for we know that they help us develop endurance. And endurance develops strength of character, and character strengthens our confident hope of salvation."* NLT

2 Corinthians 4:17 *"For our present troubles are small and won't last very long. Yet they produce for us a glory that vastly outweighs them and will last forever!"* NLT

Week 6, Day 3: Depression

Psalm 30:11 *"You have turned my mourning into joyful dancing. You have taken away my clothes of mourning and clothed me with joy, that I might sing praises to you and not be silent. O Lord my God, I will give you thanks forever."* NLT

Since my mid-teens, I have battled depression. There are seasons of life, I have discovered, that are harder than others, and there are certain circumstances that cause it to rear its ugly head. Each time my symptoms are the same, though. Sleeping, crying, a feeling of hopelessness, and feelings of uselessness all seem to crowd my time and mind. I despise how it makes me feel, and I despise even more its effect on my family. They don't deserve it, and I hate that my kids have seen it. As I began my transformation journey, emotions naturally were packed for the ride. Fears, uncertainties, and doubts crowded in and tagged along. I noticed though that as I started to lose weight, past the first 20 pounds, that my hormones and emotions started to change. I researched this, and learned that hormones are actually stored in fat. When fat is lost, those hormones release, and it actually causes problems. For me, one day I was sad, the next day I was on a cloud. I never seemed to know what tomorrow held. Over time, though, as I stayed the course, those emotions leveled out, and I battle less with depression now.

It's been a long-standing opinion with medical professionals that exercise helps ward off depression. I've found it true in my own life that when I started to feel anxiety crowding in, I go jump on the bike or the treadmill and work it out. But don't get me wrong. I don't feel like exercising in those times; in fact, it's the last thing I want to do. While I'm exercising though, I tell God all about it. It's been in those times too that God has come and spoken directly to my heart. In fact, an insecurity that I'd felt for the last 20 years was settled with God on a spin bike. Because of those times, it's made me turn to God and healthy practices when I start seeing the signs of depression.

In this 30th Psalm, David expresses his deep dependence upon God in both strong and uncertain times. He confesses his arrogance and self-sufficient attitude when times are good, but when the tables are turned, he is broken. But he cries out to God for help and pleads for the Lord's mercy. We don't know the reason for David's lament here, but he says he faced death. Whether figuratively or literally, we aren't sure, but we do know that David was in terrible distress.

But then true to His nature, God restores David and He turns David's *"mourning into joyful dancing."* And he offers his praise to God, as He truly deserves.

I've seen a common thread of depression in today's society. I'm constantly astonished and amazed at the number of people who undergo treatment for it as well as those who suffer in solitude. Let me offer hope. Jesus is there. No matter the circumstances you face, whether they seem hopeless or never-ending, He is there. Secondly, there are physical steps we can take. Physical exercise is always key to me. And if it's necessary, reach out for help to a pastor, trusted friend, or a Christian counselor. At any rate, make sure that person points you to Jesus, the only One who can bring us pure joy.

As I've traversed the season of getting healthy, I've noticed my bouts of depression grow less and less. I can't help but think that in my case, it's because through this time, I've grown closer to Him, and I've taken care of my body.

Have you ever struggled with depression? Signs and symptoms vary from person to person, and the severity and the causes are also different. Seek out help. Lean on Jesus, and get moving!

Encouragement for Today
1 Peter 5:7 *"Give all your worries and cares to God, for he cares about you."* NLT

John 10:10 *"The thief's purpose is to steal and kill and destroy. My purpose is to give them a rich and satisfying life."* NLT

Psalm 34:17-18 *"The Lord hears his people when they call to him for help. He rescues them from all their troubles. The Lord is close to the brokenhearted; he rescues those who spirits are crushed."* NLT

Disclaimer: I am not a doctor, nor do I have any medical training whatsoever. Depression is a symptom sometimes of a medical condition which should be treated by a doctor.

Week 6, Day 4: Seeing Results

Luke 8:15 *"And the seeds that fell on the good soil represents honest, good-hearted people who hear God's word, cling to it, and patiently produce a huge harvest."* NLT

I saw the number on the scale, and I saw the size on the tags, but I didn't see anything different in the mirror. The scale number was dropping, and so was my clothing size, but I honestly didn't see any huge change. Obviously, no one else did either, or so it seemed. Those that were close to me knew the journey I was on, but acquaintances that only saw me every so often didn't say a word. In fact, I had lost 50 pounds before my Sunday School teacher noticed. I know, I know, it's petty to need affirmation from other people, but I did notice that I didn't have it. Maybe they don't see a difference either, I thought. What would I have to do in order to feel like I was an "average" size?

Since that time, I've gotten a lot of positive recognition of my hard work, sometimes to the point of embarrassment. But each time, it was encouraging to know that others noticed my hard work. And it reminded me that I had changed, even if I couldn't see it myself. The only time I noticed a change in my body size was when I saw a photo of myself. Odd, isn't it?

The parable of the farmer scattering seed is a picture of God's Word being preached to the world. Some people receive the word but quickly turn back to old ways once trials come. Some people hang on for a while with God but eventually when they haven't grown, they too fall away. But others receive God's word, nourish it in their souls, grow, and then they produce a great harvest. But those who produce that great harvest must be patient and attentive to the seeds being sown. God's Word is vast and deep and calls us to a lifetime of learning. We must never stop growing and never stop sharing His Word. In due season, not only will we bear fruit for God but we will compel others as well. His Word tells us special and precious promises that He will never leave us, and He will walk beside us every day if only we are faithful. He loves us so extravagantly that He sent His only Son to be the sacrifice for our sin. How can we not receive His Word, His love letter to us and cultivate it within our souls?

As we walk with God, sometimes we don't evidently see the growth that's happening until someone else points it out. We may not see it, but rest assured, others will. They're watching, needing to see what God can do in your heart, and in theirs.

Physically speaking, as we grow stronger and healthier, we may not see much change occurring. It may be frustrating and discouraging if we allow our focus to drift away from His Word and His love for us. But in due season, we will reap a harvest. He has promised, and He is faithful!

Are you seeing visible results yet? Have your results been less than what you'd hoped for? Give it time. God's got a wonderful harvest of results waiting for you if you will only cultivate it. Keep working. You're doing great! Take some time today to read the entire parable. Which soil are you?

Encouragement for Today
Matthew 6:33 *"Seek the Kingdom of God above all else, and live righteously, and he will give you everything you need."* NLT

I can't seem to loose the few pounds that I desire + no one has noticed the few pds I have lost. But I don't really expect any one to notice. I just want to not be so conscious of the bulges I do have, be less aware of my over laps + thus be less self conscious + self focused.
I feel I can be patient at this time. Mainly cause I'm not trying as hard as I should - to exercise + eat less etc.

81

Week 6, Day 5: Plateaus

Hebrews 11:1-3 *"What is faith? It is the confident assurance that what we hope for is going to happen. It is the evidence of things we cannot yet see. God gave his approval to people in days of old because of their faith. By faith we understand that the entire universe was formed at God's command, that what we now see did not come from anything that can be seen."* ESV

Three weeks had passed since the scale had moved. Three weeks, in spite of my constant exercise and conscientious eye on my nutrition, and I hadn't lost any more weight. I was frustrated, confused, and worried that my worst fears had really come to fruition. I was just destined to be fat forever. But I pressed on, knocking my intensity up a notch, and eventually, the scale started moving again. And it moved continuously until I reached my goal.

I've heard many people talk about reaching weight-loss plateaus, but I didn't really understand it until I myself experienced it. Basically, your body becomes acclimated to your new lifestyle and refuses to let go of any weight. Eventually, if you press on, you'll start losing again. But be patient. This is quite normal, and some people even experience it more than once. Typically, this is the point when most people quit out of frustration and maybe a little boredom too. I wasn't going to be most people. I was in this for the long haul, and I wasn't going to stop until I reached my destination.

The writer of Hebrews breaks into this section of living by faith. Known as the faith chapter, he presents a long list of people like Abel, Enoch, and Abraham, who lived by faith alone and pleased God.

Faith is a tricky thing. It's having full confidence and assurance that what God has promised will come to fruition, no matter what. It's not based on our abilities and strengths; it's based on Him. Period. Putting our faith in Him requires a mental assent, but it also requires us to act based upon what God has already revealed about His will. We walk in obedience, but we walk in faith, with full confidence that what He says is true. The confidence of that faith is that we serve a God who fulfills His promises.

Sometimes it's easy to become confused and disheartened when it looks like things aren't happening and aren't progressing. But God is always at work. Remember, He never sleeps! Even when we can't see progression in our bodies or on the scale, He is still there, transforming and remaking you. He is faithful!

What has He promised you? Over and over again in Scripture, He promises to be with us, to never leave or forsake us (Matthew 28:28), and to meet our needs (Philippians 4:19). He promises that He will save us when we call on Him (Mark 16:16), and that He has prepared a place for us to be with Him someday (John 14:2-3). He has promised that He makes all things work together for our good if we love Him (Romans 8:28).

What other promises of His work do you lean upon? Take some time today to explore these and other Scriptures that He has given us as we walk in faith, confident of Him.

Encouragement for Today
Matthew 21:22 *"And whatever you ask in prayer, you will receive, if you have faith."* ESV

Mark 11:22-24 *"And Jesus answered them, "Have faith in God. Truly, I say to you, whoever says to this mountain, 'Be taken up and thrown into the sea,' and does not doubt in his heart, but believes that what he says will come to pass, it will be done for him. Therefore I tell you, whatever you ask in prayer, believe that you have received it, and it will be yours."* ESV

I believe, help my unbelief! I am also at a plateau — And that that maybe I am just destined to stay here, but I will press on. I certainly haven't been super diligent, but think maybe next week, I will be — Buck up Su & be diligent!

83

Week 6, Day 6: Vacation and Travel

Psalm 121:8 *"The Lord keeps watch over you as you come and go, both now and forever."* NLT

We were going to Disney World. Ahhh!!!! I was definitely excited, but I was also definitely nervous. I'd been to Disney World before, and the highlight of that trip had been the food. If you've never been, the food there is not your typical theme park food. There are professional chefs at all of the restaurants, and we were on the dining plan! That meant that we could eat to our heart's content. There were no limits. And what's more, I am frugal. Having paid so much money, I only felt it reasonable to eat what we had paid for. What would I do? This was my first vacation trip and I was very apprehensive about how I would balance my frugality with my healthy eating habits.

Preparation was key. Once again, I went online to find out as much information as possible on the restaurants we would be visiting. I planned my meals, my snacks, and lucky for me, there are plenty of healthy options at Disney World. I also wore a pedometer, so that I could accurately log my activity and ensure that I was on track with my nutrition. The only setback was that we were flying, and extended travel always makes me retain water. That wasn't a big deal as I would lose that added weight once we got home.

We did go on our trip, and magically (just like Disney), I managed to lose 3 pounds while we were on vacation! I couldn't believe it myself. It was possible, and it definitely is doable.

While there are definite challenges to eating healthy while on vacation and traveling in general, it is absolutely possible. With a little preparation and a lot of careful choosing, you can stick to a healthy diet. What's more, when you eat healthy food, you feel better and have more energy to do all of the fun things that you've planned.

The Psalmist here uses word pictures to assure the pilgrims spoken of here of the Lord's presence with them. Their help comes from the Lord, the one who created the heavens and the earth, as well as us, His people. He watches over them and every move they make, especially in times of trouble. The Creator stands beside them, guarding them forever.

It's a beautiful Psalm, full of compassion, love, and care for Israel. It's the same compassion, love, and care that God feels for all of us too. He cares about every move we make, our protection, our health, and even our choices we make. If we let Him, He will stand beside us, guarding us even from temptation and trouble.

Do you trust Him to take care of you and to keep you healthy even when everyone else would tell you it's okay to make bad choices? How serious are you about changing your life? Will you allow Him to guard you?

Read through the entire Psalm today. You'll be glad you did.

Encouragement for Today
Psalm 91:11 *"For he will order his angels to protect you wherever you go."* NLT

Psalm 139:9-10 *"If I ride the wings of the morning, if I dwell by the farthest oceans, even there your hand will guide me, and your strength will support me."* NLT

Just got back from a short trip to Vancouver BC and did not loose, but gain! One challenge is a husband who likes to eat out, often. It comes back to portion control if eating at places that don't have salads (oriental, thai etc.) A full spring & summer of travel, so will take much planning & discipline.

Week 6, Day 7: Sabbath Rest 6

Matthew 27:50-51 *"Then Jesus shouted out again, and he released his spirit. At that moment the curtain in the sanctuary of the Temple was torn in town, from top to bottom. The earth shook, rocks split apart."* NLT

Much of my life was spent feeling like an outsider. I was younger than the other kids in my neighborhood, and while I desperately tried to keep up, I was just smaller. As I grew older, I was always a little different. My artsy, introverted personality kept me from making many friends, and as I grew into adulthood, my classification as a woman clergy automatically labeled me as "different." In mind though, I just thought I was on the outside because I was obese. The theme throughout all of those circumstances, though, was that I was an outsider. People were generally nice to me, and things weren't all bad, but most of the time, I just wanted to blend into the wall. To this very day, I don't enjoy calling attention to myself, which makes preaching pretty tricky. There are still times that I think to myself in the middle of a sermon, "These people are looking directly at me!"

The account of the death of Jesus as recorded in Matthew tells that at the moment Jesus releases His Spirit, the veil of the Temple was torn in two, from top to bottom. In short, this veil that it speaks of served as the barrier between the Holy of Holies, the place where the Spirit of God dwelt, and the place where the Israelites worshipped. This curtain's ripping from top to bottom was important because no one but God could've done that. And secondly, we realize that now we have access to worship Him, in His very presence. Now we can go into the Holy of Holies and make our own petitions known. When the Temple veil was ripped, we knew that Jesus is our High Priest, who has made the final and ultimate sacrifice for our sins. We gained the right to worship, and we are no longer outsiders. He accepts us, just as we are because we have been bought with the precious blood of Jesus.

As we face another week, let's remember that because of Jesus, we don't have to feel that we are outsiders, alone, or less-than-desirable. His sacrifice opened the door for us to be able to worship, in the presence of Almighty God. He accepts us, and He makes us worthy.

What characteristics have you used to label yourself in the past?

Whether they're good or bad, think more of what God thinks of you. Chosen, loved, saved, creation, child...all of these are what Jesus made us by dying on the cross and defeating the grave.

Encouragement for Today
Hebrews 13:15 *"Therefore, let us offer through Jesus a continual sacrifice of praise to God, proclaiming our allegiance to his name."* NLT

Ephesians 1:4-5 *"Even as he chose us in him before the foundation of the world, that we should be holy and blameless before him. In love he predestined us for adoption as sons through Jesus Christ, according to the purpose of his will."* ESV

_____

_____

_____

_____

_____

_____

_____

_____

_____

_____

_____

_____

_____

_____

_____

Week 7, Day 1: Comparison

Philippians 2:3 *"Do nothing out of rivalry or conceit, but in humility count others more significant than yourselves."* ESV

It was my last day of work. My husband had been transferred with his job back home. I was happy about our move but sad to be leaving my job. I loved it, and I had grown to love my co-workers. They had seen me lose 45 pounds and had come to cheer me on when they realized that I was serious about getting healthy. Over time, they accepted the fact that I wasn't going to cave into temptation and triggers. I had grown here, and they had too.

Typically on our co-workers' last day, we would plan a potluck and everyone would just sort of feast all day long. It did my heart so good, though, when I walked in and everything they had brought was healthy. Obviously someone had planned this through, and they'd done it just for me. I was touched. The only problem was that they weren't sure about portion sizes, and there was a ton of food left over. Other divisions were invited over to share in the feast, and one lady in particular was so excited about the healthy options. She explained that she had been trying to lose weight and asked about my journey. After talking for a few minutes, she told me that she had lost 12 pounds in just two weeks! Wow, I thought. It took me over a month to lose that, and the pace had drastically slowed down after that first month. How had she done it? As I sat there, I knew I should be happy for her and still reveling in the sentiment that my co-workers wanted to convey, but honestly, I was just jealous.

It's been said to me that comparison is the fastest stealer of joy, and I believe it. Instead of celebrating my accomplishments and her's as well, I was just jealous inside. The green-eyed monster had won again it seemed. As I look back on that last day of work, I wish I had encouraged my co-worker to continue on and be strengthened by her initial success. Instead, I just sat quietly, sulking on the inside while trying to paste a smile on the outside. Comparison had stolen my joy.

We turn to Philippians 2 today where Paul is encouraging them to be a united body in the midst of their persecution. They were facing hard trials, and in order to get through them, they must stick together! There was encouragement found in the sole fact that they were linked together to Christ. No matter what had already happened or what was ahead, the fact that they were in Christ was enough reason to celebrate His provision. The Philippians were inspired to share and to think of others in the same way that they thought of their own interests. In that way, the body of Christ would be stronger and better able to withstand those hard trials that were coming their way.

As Christians, we all face obstacles and challenges periodically in life. Sometimes it seems that those times are never ending, but we have one another to depend on. We are not rivals with one another; we are brothers and sisters in Christ. We don't have to compare our progress with someone else's because our lives do not run parallel. But we can draw strength from one another's experiences and grow from those times! Thank God that He saw fit to place us in community where we can grow together.

Comparison is the fastest stealer of joy. But encouragement is the sole restorer of it.

How will you uplift another today that may be struggling with making healthy and right choices? How will you be encouraged by someone else who has had success? Instead of allowing jealousy to envelope you, learn all you can and be strengthened!

Encouragement for Today
Galatians 6:4 *"Pay careful attention to your own work, for then you will get the satisfaction of a job well done, and you won't need to compare yourself to anyone else."* NLT

2 Timothy 2:15 *"Work hard so you can present yourself to God and receive his approval. Be a good workers, one who does not need to be ashamed and who correctly explains the word of truth."* NLT

Yes, I am guilty of being jealous. It seems easier for Sara Green to loose 12 pds than for me to loose 1. But I am very happy for her. I know that I haven't been diligent é exercising + reducing portions.

89

Week 7, Day 2: Celebrating Victories

Psalm 126:2 *"We are filled with laughter and we sang for joy. And the other nations said, 'What amazing things the Lord has done for them.'"* NLT

A woman from my neighborhood was trying to lose weight too. We'd initially talked over our goals with one another, and she'd decided that she too would set short-term attainable goals. But she decided that at every 10 pound weight loss, she would celebrate with an all-out cheat day. Whatever she wanted, donuts, french fries, or ice cream..it was her's. She reasoned that she wouldn't have a weekly cheat meal, but after a ten-pound weight loss, she deserved it, right?

After her first ten pound weight loss, she held her much-anticipated cheat day. She had planned for two weeks what she would eat, and she enjoyed every bite. Unfortunately, the next day when she stepped back on the scale, she had gained three pounds. Although, she quickly lost those three pounds, it took longer to lose the next 20 pounds. She decided that to celebrate this victory, she would simply have 1 cheat meal. She enjoyed this meal too. But unfortunately, the next day when she stepped on the scale, she had gained weight again. After her third 10-pound weight loss, she decided that she'd choose a healthier way to celebrate.

When the Lord rescued Israel from exile and brought them back home, they celebrated! It closely mirrored the rescue of God's people out of slavery in Egypt. The radical change that had taken place for them turned them from crying and weeping to rejoicing and laughter. There was certainly reason to celebrate! The Lord had done great things for them, and they couldn't help but express their joy. The Psalmist goes onto record their prayer that God would restore their fortunes as they "plant in tears" but will harvest "with shouts of joy."

As we think of our spiritual lives, there will be times of weeping as it seems as though we are in exile. Troubles come, storms rage, and it seems as though God is absent. It is in those times though that we press in closer to God, crying out in faith that He is there, even when it doesn't seem so. In time, the storms will clear, the sun will come out, and we will rejoice that He has brought a season of harvest.

90

It's hard too when we transform our physical lives. Changes in any way are a hard adjustment, but physical ones may seen unnatural and awkward. We too may "plant in tears," but we have the hope that we will harvest "with shouts of joy." Celebrations are tricky. It's true that in biblical times, celebrations often included feasts, but they also included other forms of merriment. Dancing, singing, and fellowship were all common in praising God for the blessings they enjoyed.

When we reach weight loss goals, we should celebrate, but there are healthy ways to do it! And we must remember who gave us the strength to achieve our goal! We must praise and thank Him first of all, for leading and guiding us every step of the way. Secondly, we must be reminded that a transformed life doesn't celebrate a change by resorting to old ways. An alcoholic certainly wouldn't celebrate sobriety by having a drink to celebrate. What makes perfect sense in our old way of living suddenly seems odd when we are transformed.

Think of ways you can celebrate the victories God has given you. For me, I celebrated weight loss goals by rewarding myself by buying a new outfit or going on a weekend biking trip with my family. In whatever way you give praise and thanks to God, make sure it includes healthy shouts of joy!

Encouragement for Today
Ecclesiastes 3:4 *"A time to cry and a time to laugh, A time to grieve and a time to dance."* NLT

_____

_____

_____

_____

_____

_____

_____

Week 7, Day 3: Falling Off the Wagon

1 John 2:1 *"My dear children, I am writing this to you so that you will not sin. But if anyone does sin, we have an advocate who pleads our case before the Father. He is Jesus Christ, the one who is truly righteous. He himself is the sacrifice that atones for our sins--and not only our sins but the sins of all the world."* NLT

After a heated conversation with my boss, I was physically exhausted and emotionally drained. The last thing on my agenda was to cook a healthy meal, complete with julienned vegetables and perfectly grilled meat. That's what I had planned to do when I'd left that morning for work. All I wanted to do now was eat. I was hungry, and cooking the meal I'd planned would've taken an hour. What were we to do? We drove 20 miles and ate a fried catfish dinner, complete with french fries, onion rings, coleslaw, hush puppies, fried green tomatoes, and ice cream topped chocolate cobbler. It was good. And it got my mind off of my troubles for a solid 30 minutes. But now I felt even more miserable than before. I was guilty of trying to drown my wounded emotions with deep-fried fat, and now I had to deal with it.

Days are not always going to be easy, and unfortunately, there will be times when we "fall off the wagon." The great thing is, we can learn from these mistakes, and also, there are actually a few things we can do to counter the times when we indulge. First of all, make sure that you hit or exceed your water goal for the day, particularly if you've consumed a lot of salty foods. Water will go a long way to flush out your system. Secondly, make sure you also meet or exceed your fiber goal. Fiber attaches itself to fat and flushes it right out of your system.

Turning back to bad habits, even for a day can be detrimental to your healthy lifestyle. Besides the nutritional de-railings of calorie counts, the side effects of fat/sugar-laden foods and added temptations can hang on for days at a time. The goal of healthy living is that these instances don't occur at all, but at times, they do.

In our Scripture today, we read of John's passion to call believers to live a life above sin. The purpose of chapter 1 is to draw us away from sin and to avoid it altogether. But chapter 2, begins by saying, "But if anyone does sin..." There it is. The intent of our hearts is to be that we avoid it at all costs, but unfortunately, there are times that the enemy prowls, and we give in. When that happens, Jesus stands as our Advocate, representing us to the Father. We don't have to be afraid to confess and repent of our sins because Christ is there. When God raised Jesus Christ from the grave, He accepted Christ's sacrifice in our place.

As we travel on in our journey to be healthier physically and spiritually, take comfort in knowing that our trip isn't over when we "fall off the wagon." We can get back up and travel on.

What actions have you take when you've been derailed? Do you get back up and keep going or do you backtrack to old ways?

Encouragement for Today
1 John 1:9 *"But if we confess our sins to him, he is faithful and just to forgive us our sins and to cleanse us from all wickedness."* NLT

This is so true. One indulgent leads to more, not recording my intake, leads to more days 5. But I think I fall off the wagon less often recently. Thank you Lord.

My biggest issue right now is large servings. I don't need that much food, I eat it cause its there, + its good!

Week 7, Day 4: Stress

Philippians 4:6 *"Be careful for nothing; but in every thing by prayer and supplication with thanksgiving let your requests be made known unto God."* KJV

About the time I was winding down my weight-loss journey with only 10 pounds to go, my husband was transferred with his job out of state. We were moving 400 miles away, and we had to find a house, buy it, wrap up our jobs, say goodbye to strong friendships, and move, all within 4 weeks. It was stressful to say the least, especially considering our mortgage lender and our realtor's staff seemed not too concerned with our tight deadline. What was quickly promised as "totally doable" when we communicated our moving date, suddenly was "highly unlikely," the closer our date came. Every day, and sometimes multiple times a day, during that 4 weeks, I had to call the lender and the realtor to find out where we were in the process. And sure enough, when the day came to load the moving truck, we still weren't sure of the exact closing date. We were driving our entire lives across 400 miles with what was actually, nowhere to go. We were homeless. The closing date came and passed without signed papers, and I was stressed to the max. Everything we owned sat in a truck in my parents' driveway for days until we signed those papers. We ended up closing two days late, and I was livid.

During that time, I gained 5 pounds. What was supposed to be a very delicate time of losing the last 10, ended up stress-filled. Even though I closely monitored my activity and nutrition, it was to no avail. The stress hormone had won, and I was its culprit. Stress keeps us from losing weight and can actually cause us to gain it.

As a very high-strung person, stress is my weakness. I always feel like I have broad shoulder, and I can handle most problems myself. That personality trait tends though to harm me and actually, hinder my relationship with Jesus. He desires to handle our stress for us, but when we refuse to let it go, it does nothing but hurt us.

In this section of Paul's letter to the Philippians, he addresses a small conflict that has arisen in the church. He encourages them to work through their disagreement and to allow God to free them from their worry. We must rejoice, he says and to be full of the joy of the Lord. Further, he says not to worry, pray, and be thankful. There it is. It's the formula for less-stress living.

Troubles arise, and there are seasons of life that naturally bring stress. Any change in life whatsoever can bring about stress, even in small amounts. But God doesn't want us to live this way, and He can alleviate it, if we give it to Him. God loves us, His children, and doesn't want us to worry about anything. He cares about our needs and invites us to talk to Him about everything.

What's troubling you today? What causes stress in your life? Take some time to read through this chapter and pray about those things. He can handle them!

Encouragement for Today
John 14:27 *"Peace I leave with you, my peace I give unto you; not as this world giveth, give I unto you. Let not your heart be troubled, neither let it be afraid."* KJV

Psalm 55:22 *"Cast thy burden upon the Lord, and he shall sustain thee: he shall never suffer the righteous to be moved."* KJV

I praise God that I am not experiencing big time stress right now. It doesn't take much + my adrenaline ↑. Thank you Lord for only the small stresses. But even those, I need to turn to God to manage.

Week 7, Day 5: Bad Day

Psalm 50:15 *"Then call on me when you are in trouble, and I will rescue you, and you will give me glory."* NLT

Today didn't start well. Yesterday, our Mississippi hometown got an unprecedented 9 inches of snow. To some reading this, it isn't a big deal, but you see, our town doesn't own snow-removal equipment. And it certainly doesn't have a plan in place to deal with it. Yesterday was all fun as we played in the snow, watched movies, made a pot of chili, and played board games, but today, it's time to dig out and go back to work. I wasn't thrilled about driving in it, and I was worried about my husband leaving for work so early before the sun rose.

Our typically outside pet slept in the garage last night due to the temps, and well...when you gotta go, you gotta go. My husband didn't realize that he stepped in...well, ya know...and he tracked it all over the house...on my new carpet! Trying to deal with the amount of snow on our car, he also tracked snow all over the house. There's nothing like being in your yoga pants, barefooted in your nice warm house and suddenly stepping in snow-covered poop....on your new carpet!

My 13-year old daughter thought all of this was funny. She also thought it was funny when I discovered that two peppermints had been washed and dried with a load of laundry, and now the entire load was covered in a sugary goo. I didn't think it was funny. And I let her know. Trying to shampoo carpet at 7:00 a.m., I was grouchy, grumbly, I could feel my rising heart rate, and I hadn't even stepped foot on the treadmill!

"Jesus!," I cried out, "I need Jesus now!" To which my daughter responded, "Yes, you do!" I didn't think this was funny either. I looked at my now-cold previously scrambled eggs, and in that moment, all I wanted was a donut...or two or three, nice and hot.

My homeschooled children were sitting at the dining room table waiting for me to start our morning devotion, and I realized that I was in no shape in that moment to share the Word with anyone and expect great results.

So I turned in my Bible to Psalm 50. The psalmist writes of God's judgment as he reminds both the godly and the ungodly that God doesn't necessarily need our rituals, sacrifices, and outward signs of devotion. He owns the world, and all that is in it. What he wants is changed hearts and lives. I was immediately convicted about my attitude, my words, and the way I had treated my family. I certainly hadn't been the kind of encouraging wife or mother they needed to see as they started their day. And I felt failure. But then hope renewed when I read verse 15, *Then call on me when you are in trouble, and I will rescue you, and you will give me glory.*

I was indeed in trouble. I was in trouble of mind, body, and spirit. But calling on Him renewed my outlook on the day. Things happen, irritating things occur, but when they do, we ask for Him to rescue us. And rescue us, He does! He loves us so extravagantly and wants the best for us, and our families, even more so than we! I want to give God glory in every area of my life, but walking around feeling defeated certainly doesn't bring Him glory.

Maybe your day is off to a bad start, and you're feeling defeated. I hope your carpet hasn't been ruined, your laundry isn't sugar-coated, and traffic isn't hazardous. Maybe you've made some mistakes today and you're feeling defeated. Take heart! Call on Him and He will rescue you, and you will bring Him glory!

Take a few moments and read the entire Psalm. Press in.

Encouragement for Today
Psalm 37:23-24 *"The steps of a man are established by the Lord, when he delights in his way; thought he fall, he shall not be cast headlong, for the Lord upholds his hand."* ESV

Philippians 3:3 *"For we are the circumcision, who worship by the Spirit of God and glory in Christ Jesus and put no confidence in the flesh."* ESV

Hebrews 11:6 *"And without faith it is impossible to please him, for whoever would draw near to God must believe that he exists and that he rewards those who seek him."* ESV

Defeat is a common feeling — all too often. I want to be God-controlled, please Lord.

97

Week 7, Day 6: Injuries

2 Corinthians 12:8-10 *"Three different times I begged the Lord to take it away. Each time he said, "My grace is all you need. My power works best in weakness." So now I am glad to boast about my weaknesses, so that the power of Christ can work through me."* NLT

The much-anticipated day had finally arrived. We had just relocated back to our home state of Mississippi, and we were finally going to get to try out the new Tanglefoot Trail. For us, it's a bike trail, but walkers, joggers, and mommies with baby strollers call it home too. There's beautiful, tranquil scenery and just enough hills and turns to make it a little challenging, which is why we love it. I'm a stickler for tracking both my nutrition and my activity, so I was keeping track of my time with my phone. We were coming upon a stop sign, and I reached to get my phone out of my bicycle pouch. I pressed the round button to power on the screen, tapped "stop" on my handy little app, and squeezed the brakes simultaneously. Yes, I did all that at the same time, while still riding the bike. The only problem is, I'm right handed, and so I was messing with my phone with my right hand while squeezing the left brake. NEVER DO THAT. Never, ever, ever squeeze your left brake unless you want to take up gymnastics. Before I knew what was happening, I flew over the handlebars, catching myself on the asphalt with both of my arms, extended, and locked. At first, I didn't think I was actually hurt, and was just worried who had just seen my less-than-graceful dismount. When I finally sat up, I could see that both of my knees, my hip, and even my forehead were skinned. Great. Now I've skinned my face. I knew something was wrong with my left arm, but it didn't look bad from the outside. I also knew that I couldn't continue on our bike ride, but we were five miles from the car, and we were in the middle of nowhere. My choices were pretty limited. We could walk back, all four of us, wheeling our bikes, or we could ride. "Are you sure you can ride?" my husband asked. "I'm in pain, and it's faster to get back to the car if we ride," I reasoned. So we rode back to the car. Convinced I only had sprained the arm, I sat in agony on the couch for five hours before my husband convinced me to go to the doctor before we were forced to sit in an ER waiting room. That made sense, and at least I would be able to sleep maybe.

"Well, you've broken your arm," the doctor stated. I was shocked. I've never broken a bone in my body, I thought. There's truly a first time for everything, I guess. The second thought I mulled was how I was going to keep working out while my arm healed. This was inconvenient, and it definitely wasn't in my plan. I had momentum, and I aimed to finish my weight loss journey. On time.

Paul writes in this letter about the famous thorn in his side. We don't know exactly what the thorn was, but it doesn't matter. He had difficulties, plain and simple, that he says were put there to keep him from being self-sufficient. The analogy of the thorn was used to prick the balloon of pride. Therefore, he boasted in his weaknesses, so that Christ's power would be made evident. Because God is enough, we need not become overwhelmed when obstacles stand in our way. We need only see them as opportunities for God's strength to shine through.

When we're in the middle of physical training, injuries can be so frustrating and untimely. And they are always untimely. But there are ways to work around them and through them. If we allow it, we can learn something new and embrace the opportunity to lean on Him, instead of our own strength.

What's the obstacle you're facing today? Take some time and fill in the journal area. On one side, list the hurdles you may be facing. And then on the other side, make a list of everything you know to be true about God. I guarantee you the second column will be longer. He is enough. And his power works best when we are weak.

Encouragement for Today
Romans 8:28 *"And we know that God causes everything to work together for the good of those who love God and are called according to his purpose for them."* NLT

Hurdles I am Facing	What I know about God	
flu & cold	Provides power to	obstain
Gary & eating out	Answers prayer	
Not accessing God's power	Encourages	
	Provided scripture	to
Plateaus & no wt. loss	remind of promises	
Interference c work outs	Provides friends to	come
	along side.	

Week 7, Day 7: Sabbath Rest 7

Isaiah 43:18-19 *"But forget all that--it is nothing compared to what I am going to do. For I am about to do a brand-new thing. See, I have already begun! Do you not see it? I will make a pathway through the wilderness for my people to come home. I will create rivers for them in the desert!"* NLT

Once I started to lose weight, I started feeling different. I had no idea that I felt so bad when I was obese. The energy increase, better breathing, and confidence was like propeller to me, causing me to look forward to the future for the first time in a long time. As I enjoyed living inside my new body, I realized all of the time I had wasted, living unhappy and unhealthy. The time of my life that should've been spent full of activity and socialization, my teens and 20's, were spent inside, afraid of other people. Years went by without anyone taking a photo of me with my children simply because I hated to look at myself in pictures. I banned anyone from tagging me in photos on social media as well, simply because I wouldn't have a chance to edit or approve of the picture beforehand. Regret filled me, even though I should've been excited about losing weight. Finally, I was starting to get healthy, and I actually had a figure, but all I felt was regret.

That's why I love the 43rd chapter of Isaiah. In it, Isaiah reminds the people of Israel of all the things God has done for them and all the things that He's brought them through. He rescued them from Egypt, and He carried them through the Red Sea on dry ground. He was faithful through all of the hard times, but they themselves were not always faithful. God has been there, guiding and leading them through it all, but He's not done yet. Rather than living in the past, God wanted them to look forward to the future in faith. He is still the same faithful God. In the beginning of the next chapter, in fact, Isaiah reminds them of their sins of all the ages, but God is doing something new! They can walk forward into the future confident that God will bless them, His very own people!

As I walked into the future, I couldn't help but take a peek at the past, of all of the ways God has led me and has been faithful. Even in times of sadness and despair, I can see His hand was at work the entire time. He never left me, even when I felt alone. I caused years of undue hardship on myself simply because I wasn't willing to let go of the physical aspect of my spiritual relationship. When I didn't care for my body the way God desired, it prevented me from living a life of full freedom in Him.

Today, I'm excited that God desires to do something new in my life. I have a new body, a new vision for the future, and I am unhindered in the ways I can minister for His kingdom. In all of the ways that I felt handicapped before, I can now share His healing with others. As Isaiah said, He made a pathway for me when I was in the wilderness to come home to Him. He has done a new thing in me, and I see it clearly!

What is God doing right now in your life? Are you living in regrets and guilt of the past? Allow God to transform you life, and refuse to waste another second living a life sub-par to the one God has in store for you. His ways are better than ours, and His plans are far more exciting! He is indeed doing something new in you. Walk on your path through the wilderness to come home to Him. He is waiting!

Make a list today of all the things God has done for you and brought you through.

Encouragement for Today
2 Corinthians 7:10 *"For the kind of sorrow God wants us to experience leads us away form sin and results in salvation. There's no regret for that kind of sorrow. But worldly sorrow, which lacks repentance, results in spiritual death."* NLT

Joel 2:25 *"I will repay you for the years the locusts have eaten..."* NIV

Regret has always been an issue in my life - big - what, I say, impressions things + little - events, neglects etc. I truelly desire freedom from that constant tendency. I waste energies ē regretting. I need to forgive myself + move on.

Made in the USA
San Bernardino, CA
30 November 2016